Do Angels Really Exist?

Separating Fact from Fantasy

by Dr. David O. Dykes

Huntington House Publishers

Huntington House Publishers
P.O. Box 53788
Lafayette, Louisiana 70505

Library of Congress Card Catalog Number 95-
78013
ISBN 1-56384-105-3

Printed in the U.S.A.

*All Scripture is taken from the
New International Version (NIV)
of the Bible, unless otherwise indicated.*

Dedication

Dedicated to
Jennifer Christian and Laura Grace
who will always be their dad's
"little angels."
Even when they aren't,
they still are.

Contents

Preface   ix

Section I
The Mystery of Angels

Chapter 1
  Angels, Angels, Everywhere!   13

Chapter 2
  Fantasy or Fact about Angels?   19

Section II
Jesus: The Master of Angels

Chapter 3
  Angels at the Birth and
  Temptation of Jesus   45

Chapter 4
  Jesus Taught about Angels   53

Chapter 5
  Angels at the Death and
  Resurrection of Jesus   65

v

Chapter 6
Angels and the Second Coming **67**

Section III
The Ministry of Angels

Chapter 7
Angels Pronounce God's
Message to Us **75**

Chapter 8
Angels Provide for Our Needs **81**

Chapter 9
Angels Protect Us from Harm **89**

Chapter 10
Angels Preside at Our Death **113**

Chapter 11
Angels Praise God with Us **121**

Section IV
The Might of Angels

Chapter 12
The Army of Angels **127**

Chapter 13
An Army of Divisions **133**

Chapter 14
An Army of Destruction **139**

Chapter 15
An Army of Deliverance   **145**

Section V
The Message of Angels

Chapter 16
Afraid? Cheer Up!   **155**

Chapter 17
Sleeping? Wake Up!   **165**

Chapter 18
Silent? Speak Up!   **173**

Preface

Every book is the product of many helpful people. I have been blessed by the generous help of many precious friends.

Thank you to Arlene Huckaby who is more than my secretary. She is more than my right-hand person. She is like an iron lung for me—I couldn't live without her. She has cheerfully typed and retyped this manuscript to get it ready to publish.

Thanks also to Carye Gillen who devoted many hours to sifting through the many "angel encounters" to select the very best ones to appear in this book. She also helped in improving the format of the chapters.

Blessings to Dr. Rita Bryant for her editorial proofreading which isolated all the split infinitives, double negatives, and any other grammatical faux pas.

A million thanks go to my wonderful wife, Cindy, who not only first got me interested in angels, but also encouraged me for years to write this book.

My gratitude goes out to the hundreds of individuals who submitted angel encounters to me. I'm still receiving good ones. If you think you've "entertained an angel," write me through the publisher and tell me about it.

Section I
The Mystery of Angels

In a world of flesh and blood, there is something mysterious about the idea that invisible, spiritual beings exist around us.

However, the history and folklore of every culture makes mention of "spirits." A careful study of what the Bible says about angels will remove the mystery and allow us to accept their wonderful ministry in our lives.

Chapter 1

Angels, Angels, Everywhere!

Folklore, Hollywood, and imagination have given us many strange ideas about angels: who they are, where they reside, and what they do. These popular beliefs are often more fiction than truth. I invite you to put aside all such false ideas and join us as we focus upon what God's Word, the Bible, tells us about these special, supernatural helpers.

I first became fascinated with angels a few years ago when I read Billy Graham's excellent book, *Angels: God's Secret Agents*. In my opinion, this remains the finest book on the subject. In his book, Dr. Graham relates the story of missionary John Pollock and his wife who went to the New Hebrides Islands in the South Pacific. When they arrived, they were the first white missionaries that the natives had ever seen. The witch doctor was afraid of the Pollocks and told the tribe that the missionaries had come to kill the babies of the tribe. So, on the first evening the natives surrounded the hut of John and his wife, preparing to kill them. All night long the missionaries stayed on their knees in prayer.

The native warriors never attacked. As time passed, the missionaries learned the language and won the trust of the people. Many of them came to know Christ.

After the chief of the tribe became a Christian, John said to him, "We have always been curious why, on that first night when you surrounded us with your spears, you didn't attack."

The native asked, "Where did you get all of those men?"

John said, "It was only my wife and me."

The chief responded, "Oh, no. All that evening we saw large men with swords in their hands surrounding your hut. We were afraid and we never attacked."[1]

Billy Graham and I agree that this is just one of thousands of manifestations of God's special secret agents—His angels. In this book, you will read of many similar angelic encounters.

The most helpful Scripture about angels is found in Hebrews 1:13. Hebrews is all about the superiority of Jesus: how He is superior to angels, to Moses, and to the Law. In Hebrews 1:13–14, we read these words, "To which of the angels did God ever say, 'Sit at my right hand until I make your enemies a footstool for your feet?' Are not all angels ministering spirits sent to serve those who will inherit salvation?"

---

[1]Billy Graham, *Angels: God's Secret Agents* (Garden City, NY: Doubleday and Company, Inc., 1975), 3.

This is a concise statement that reveals the identity and purpose of angels. They are spirits sent to serve the saints. Out of His gracious concern for us, our Father sends His angels to assist us. If you ask me, "Have you ever encountered an angel?" I would answer that I believe that I have. You will read later about some of my "angel encounters." If you ask me whether I have ever physically seen an angel, I would have to say to you, "I'm not sure." I hope that you, too, are not sure. Why? In the last chapter of Hebrews, there is a fascinating passage of Scripture that tells us that we might have encountered angels and not even been aware of them. In Hebrews 13:2, we read, "Do not forget to entertain strangers, for by so doing some people have entertained angels without knowing it." The King James version says, "entertained angels unaware." You might have encountered angels and not even known it, and I might have as well. I hope you will keep an open mind about angels. I also hope you will keep your eyes open as you begin to look for angelic activity around you.

When it comes to the subject of angels, people seem to be divided into two extremes. On one hand, most people seem to be ignorant about angels. On the other hand, a growing number of people are becoming obsessed with the topic of angels.

Is Ignorance Bliss?

Which of these two categories do you fit into? I confess that for much of my Christian life I was totally ignorant of angels. I grew up in a wonderful, Bible-preaching Baptist church. Although I went to Sunday School and to worship services on Sundays and Wednesdays, I can't ever recall hearing a single sermon on angels. I went to a major Baptist university where I majored in religion. I don't remember ever hearing any of my religion professors teaching about angels. After college, I did seven years of post-graduate work. During the seven years that I was in the seminary, I never heard one professor say anything about angels.

Several years ago, I consulted my books on systematic theology. In the index, there was not even a listing for angels. Isn't this lack of teaching about angels rather strange? There almost seems to be a satanic strategy to keep God's people in the dark about the wonderful subject of angels.

After reading Billy Graham's book, I became so interested in angels that I conducted an intense study on the topic. My computer has a Bible concordance; and several years ago, I searched every verse that mentioned angels, spirits, or cherubs. I was shocked when my printer scrolled out forty pages of single-spaced references to angels. There were almost five hundred Scriptures! I was not aware that the Bible had that much to say about angels. There is no excuse for a Christian to be ignorant about angels.

An Unhealthy Obsession

While many people know virtually nothing about the subject, there are people who have become so enchanted with angels that their interest has become an obsession. Secular America is fascinated with angels. *USA Today* has featured cover stories about angels. The *Ladies Home Journal* printed an article on them as well. Sophie Burnham has published two best-selling books, one entitled *The Angel Book* and the other *Angel Letters*. Much of the secular world is entranced with the mystery of angels.

Many writers are communicating misconceptions and much misunderstanding regarding angels. For example, the New Age religion has gladly embraced the concept of angels. With an anything-goes attitude, New Agers have stepped over the line of truth and have started talking about the "angel within." They talk about "getting in touch with their angel," which to them, may be the same as "a channeling spirit." This confusion has misled many sincere people into faulty thinking about angels. Some have even been led into the dangerous practice of spiritism, believing they can communicate with the dead.

In addition to intellectual interest, there is great commercial interest in angels. There is an angel store in Denver, Colorado, that is ready to franchise across America. The name of the store is Everything Angels. You will probably see this chain of stores spread to many malls. Apparently, business is brisk in the sale of angels and angel pins. The idea is trendy, a fad, leading some people to become obsessed with the popularity of angels.

As with many spiritual issues, the truth remains between these two extremes. Let's not be ignorant about angels. Let's learn what the Bible says about them, but let's not develop obsessive behavior concerning them. Angels are so much more than porcelain figures or golden lapel pins. They are special spirits sent to serve God's children.

Chapter 2

Fantasy or Fact about Angels?

When I am searching for the truth about
any issue, I look first in the Bible. I am basi-
cally a biblical Christian. That means, where
the Bible speaks, I speak with certainty. Where
the Bible is silent, I am silent. To find the truth
about angels, you must open your heart to
believe what God's Word says, not what you
read in the secular media. Don't always swallow
what an individual says happened to him concerning an angel encounter, unless the experience coincides with what God's Word says about
angels. Let's separate the fantasy from the facts.
In this chapter, we will examine five of the
fantasies about angels, then we will compare and
contrast them to the biblical facts about angels.

> FANTASY: Angels are human beings
>   who have died.
> BIBLICAL FACT: Angels are spiritual
>   beings created by God.

Where did we get the notion that angels are
human beings who have died, gone to heaven,

19

and acquired wings? The idea has been promoted for years through folk tales, popular fiction, and the movies.

Each Christmas I watch *It's A Wonderful Life* because I love it. It's one of the most popular movies of all time. Jimmy Stewart plays George Bailey, a good man who finds himself in deep financial trouble. In his depression, he poises on the edge of a snow-covered bridge. He has decided to jump into the icy water and take his life so that his family can benefit from his life insurance policy.

At precisely the right moment, his guardian angel appears to rescue him from suicide. Henry Traver plays Clarence, a somewhat goofy guardian angel. Clarence has been assigned to save George Bailey and to prove to him that life would be less-than-wonderful without him. You know the rest of the story. Clarence, a guy who died in the 1800s, has been working for years to "earn his wings" and graduate from being a second-class angel. Only by helping George can he become an "angel first-class."

At the climax of the movie, the grateful citizens of Bedford Falls are bringing in money to help George pay off his debts. Everyone is standing around the Christmas tree singing. Suddenly, the bell at the top of the tree rings. George's daughter, ZuZu, says, "Teacher says every time a bell rings, an angel gets his wings." Jimmy Stewart looks up and says, "That a boy, Clarence."

This is a typical example of how Hollywood unintentionally promotes false teachings about angels. It's a great story, but terrible teaching.

Sometimes, even well-meaning Christians will say something that reflects this fantasy. When their mother or father dies, they will say, "God has another angel." I know that they mean that their loved one is in heaven, but God doesn't have another angel. He has another saint who has died and gone to heaven. Sometimes a family will have a baby who dies, and they will say, "God has another little angel." That baby is indeed in heaven, but not as an angel. No, angels are not human beings who have died.

You may have read so-called angel stories that teach this fantasy. For example, a person might say, "I had an encounter with my Aunt Gertrude who passed away twelve years ago. She came to me, and she is now an angel." You can be sure that when the so-called angel is someone the speaker recognizes, it is either a deceiving spirit or the person is deceived, because angels are not human beings who have died. You never find one reference in the Bible that even suggests that a person can become an angel after he dies.

What does the Bible teach? Colossians 1:16 tells us that Jesus created everything. "For by him all things were created: things in heaven and on earth, visible and invisible, whether thrones or powers or rulers or authorities; all things were created by him and for him." The angels are those "invisible" things Jesus created. Angels are created by God.

The Bible says God knows the number of angels. How many are there? We don't know, but we believe that there is a set number. In Revelation 5:11, John records, "Then I looked and heard the voice of many angels, numbering thousands upon thousands, and ten thousand times ten thousand." That is a mind-boggling number of angels. Only God knows the exact number He created.

The Bible never mentions that angels get older. It never speaks of an angel who dies. You never see baby angels. In fact, we know from what Jesus says that angels do not reproduce. (See Mark 12:25.) He says that when we go to heaven, we will be like the angels in the sense that we won't have to marry for human procreation. So, the angels are immortal spiritual beings created by God. Free your mind from the fantasy that they are loved ones who died and who are trying to earn their wings.

> FANTASY: Angels appear as chubby babies with wings.
> BIBLICAL FACT: Angels most often appear as ordinary men.

It is a fantasy conceived in the fertile minds of artists and storytellers that angels are chubby infants with wings. Angels are frequently depicted in paintings, books, and films as cupid-like babies who shoot romantic arrows into the hearts of lovers.

Many people enjoy collecting angel figu-
rines. My wife does, too. There is nothing wrong
with collecting these appealing objects, but I
think that when we get to see all the angels, we
may be surprised that the ceramics and the
celestial don't match in appearance. We may
fantasize that angels are rosy-cheeked babies,
with little wings, but in the Bible they usually
appear as unexceptional men. They are often
mistaken for men.

The Bible teaches that there are different
kinds of angels. In addition to the archangel
Michael, there are seraphim and cherubim.
These are described in chapter 13.

There are also what we would call, for lack
of a better term, God's holy angels. You might
want to call them ordinary angels except there
is nothing ordinary about them. They don't
have wings; they just appear as men.

When Abraham encountered three angels,
they appeared as three ordinary men. In fact,
he mistook them for men. (See Gen. 18:2.)
When Minoah, who was the father-to-be of
Samson, encountered his angel, he thought it
was merely a man. He didn't know until later
that it was an angel (Judg. 13:21). Throughout
the Bible, we read of angels simply appearing
as mortals. The only way that we know they are
angels is by the divine message they deliver. (See
Acts 1:10.) Often, they are identified because their
clothing or their faces are shining with the glory
of God.

There have been many occasions in my life where I suspect I was assisted by an angelic minister, although I haven't seen any wings, yet! One of these circumstances sticks out in my memory more than any other.

In the summer of 1993, I was leading a group of thirty-six volunteer missionaries from our church into the former Soviet Union. We were involved in singing concerts in the Russian language, passing out Russian Bibles, and doing evangelistic work. God blessed us in a tremendous way with over two thousand professions of faith during our stay.

The most difficult part of the entire trip was coordinating our travel and transportation arrangements. Staying in Moscow and using the Vnukovo airport is a genuine nightmare. This domestic airport is old-fashioned, dark, and terribly inefficient. On our way through Moscow to the Crimea, it took us several hours to get processed.

We were facing a real challenge on our return trip because we had a very short time to claim our luggage and take a bus from the Vnukovo airport to the international airport. Anyone who has visited the former Soviet Union understands our predicament.

The Russians never get in a hurry and they often have an aversion to doing things efficiently. Thankfully, on returning to Moscow, we received our luggage and boarded our bus quickly. However, we had a very tight schedule when we arrived at Sheremetyevo airport on the other side of Moscow. We quickly unloaded our bus and entered the unfamiliar, confusing scene of the massive airport. We were required to go through customs and check our baggage before we could proceed to the airline departure gate. This is a process that could have taken several hours, and our flight was leaving in less than an hour. None of our group looked forward to the prospect of missing our flight back to America. I quickly began to pray for God's help.

Try to imagine thirty-six Americans, loaded down with luggage, rushing into an unfamiliar airport where none of us spoke fluent Russian. Immediately, a middle-aged man in blue coveralls approached me and said in fairly decent English, "May I help you?" He appeared to be an airport employee.

I breathed a prayer of thanks to God and explained to the gentleman that we were on a tight schedule, trying to make a Lufthansa flight to Frankfurt, Germany. He smiled and told me to follow him.

Our convoy of people and luggage traveled down through the airport and arrived at the scene where the customs agents were tediously checking the luggage of everyone leaving Russia. My heart dropped because I knew that it would take us far too long to get through those lines to make our flight.

I was pleasantly surprised when our friend in the blue coveralls invited me to bring my group down to the far end of the customs area.

There he enlisted another customs agent, just for our group. Miraculously, our group was cleared through with very little problem. Our friend was most helpful and even returned several times to carry our luggage from the customs area to the Lufthansa counter where we checked in. He was pleasant and friendly to each member of our group. Everyone commented on his help.

After our group's luggage was checked, I looked around for our friend because I wanted to give him a tip for his help. He was nowhere to be seen. It was as if he had simply disappeared. It was an open area, impossible to find a hiding place. One moment he was there and the next moment he was gone. I walked all around the customs and check-in area and never saw him again.

I went to the airport security office and a friendly, English-speaking agent offered to assist me. I carefully explained to him about this man who had helped us and that I wanted to show our appreciation to him.

The security agent looked at me with a puzzled expression and explained that he knew of no one matching that description who worked at the airport. In fact, he said that none of their employees wore blue coveralls!

I walked back to the check-in area, shaking my head, wondering if God had provided a special "airport angel" to assist our group. To this day, I still believe that this was God's special servant, sent to help His missionaries make it back to America on time.

> FANTASY: Angels are sweet creatures
> who sing and play harps.
> BIBLICAL FACT: Angels are most often
> warriors who hold swords.

Have you ever noticed that a proud new parent will often look into the face of a newborn baby and say, "Oh, the sweet little angel." That evaluation is not based on the Bible. Angels never appear as sweet little creatures. Most often they are described as warriors who wield swords. They are fearless, mighty warriors who comprise the ranks of God's army.

The first mention of angels in the Bible is in Genesis 3 when God places the cherubim, each with a flaming sword, at the Garden of Eden to prevent Adam and Eve from returning. All throughout the Word of God we see military references used for angels. When Jesus talked about them, He said, "I could call twelve legions of angels" (Matt. 26:53). A legion is a word for a military division.

Isaiah 37:36 says that in one night, a single angel killed 185,000 soldiers. A singular angel is strong enough to defeat an entire army. Imagine what a legion of angels can do! I would encourage you to read Frank Peretti's first two novels, *This Present Darkness* and *Piercing the Darkness*. These excellent works of fiction are based on the truth of invisible spiritual warfare

going on around us. I think you will find the
books to be very good reading, and your eyes
will be opened to a whole new world of the role
of God's mighty angels.

Karen Hawthorn confirmed angels as warriors in the following encounter.

Angel Encounter
by
Karen Hawthorn

*My husband left me alone with two daugh-
ters. He left us many times, but this was
final and I knew I would have to adjust to
raising my daughters by myself. I was always
scared at night when I was by myself. We
lived on the outskirts of Seguin, and every
noise scared me. I could never sleep at night.
I paced the floor. I used to go to my baby's
crib and rock her for hours during the night.*

*I had returned to my teaching job and was
not rested after being up all night. When I
came home from school, I still had to take
care of my girls and then face the night alone.*

*I don't know how long I had been alone
when I saw my angel. During the night I was
walking "my path" around the house, going
from room to room. I passed the patio door
and barely peeked out the curtain. At the opposite corner of the concrete slab of the patio
stood my guard, in armor with a sword. I
remember closing the curtain real fast and
when I looked again he was gone. I went to*

check on the girls, and then I went to bed. I slept every night after that. I wasn't scared of nighttime any more.

I still see that guard in my mind, but I've never seen him physically again as I did that night. I have no doubts of what I saw and felt.

Do Angels Sing?

We often picture angels as gentle creatures who are only interested in singing and playing harps. Actually, the Bible never says that angels play harps. You may also be surprised to learn that the Bible never says angels sing!

A few years ago, I was reading the commentary that W.A. Criswell wrote on Revelation.[2] For over fifty years, Dr. Criswell served as esteemed pastor of First Baptist Church in Dallas. Dr. Criswell mentioned that the Bible never says angels sing. As I read that, I said to myself, "That's not true, angels do sing!" I set out to prove that Dr. Criswell's statement was wrong. Although I thoroughly researched all the Scriptures, I never found one verse that mentions the angels' singing. At Christmas, we sing "Angels we have heard on high, sweetly singing over the plains." But, the Bible never says angels sing. Look it up for yourself.

---

[2]Criswell, W.A., *Expository Sermons on Revelation*, vol. 3 (Grand Rapids, MI: Zondervan Publishing House), 82–83.

Some people look at Job 38:7, and say,
"Well, the Bible says the 'morning stars' sang
at the creation." Some believe that those are
angels. But, most commentators say that it is
just a personification of nature, as when the
Bible says, "The trees of the field shall clap
their hands" (Isa. 55:12). And, Job 38:7 says in
the very next portion of that verse, "and all the
angels shouted for joy." Angels shout praises,
but we never read of them singing.

You may be thinking, "What about the account in Luke 2, when the shepherds were out
in the field and Jesus was born? Didn't the
angelic choir sing 'glory to God in the highest
and on earth peace, good will toward men?' "
(See Luke 2:13–14.) No, we sing it in Christmas musicals, but the Bible said they spoke
those words.

One of the first verbs conjugated by Bible
students in Greek 101 is the Greek word *lego*,
which means "to speak." That is the exact word
in Luke 2:13. Most newer translations use the
correct word, *saying*. "Suddenly a great company of the heavenly host appeared with the
angel, praising God and saying" (Luke 2:13).

Dr. Criswell concedes:

> Another thing which is astonishing to me
> is that angels never sing. Never! When I
> stumbled into that fact, it was an amaz-
> ing discovery. But I have already made
> up my mind, before I say these things,
> that I am going to keep on referring to

angels singing, even though it's not true.
I'm going to speak of angels singing, the
celestial choir, the angelic hosts. But actually angels never sing.[3]

You may wonder what the significance of
this point is. I believe that according to the
Scriptures, the only people who really have the
right and responsibility to sing are God's saints,
the born-again Christians. Angels have never
been lost and never been saved. They don't
know the joy of salvation as we do. You say,
What about in Revelation? Doesn't it say that
the angels will gather around and sing to the
Lamb on the throne? Check it out. It says they
speak their praise, but the saints sing a new
song.

Revelation 4:8 speaks of the angels chant-
ing praise to the Lamb on the throne. The
Greek word is *legontas* (from the word *lego*—to
speak). However, Revelation 5:9, speaks of the
twenty-four elders singing a new song. I believe these elders represent all the redeemed
of the ages. That's what we'll be doing. Later in
the chapter, when the angels join the chorus,
the word *legontas* (to speak) is used. (See Rev.
5:12,13.) Although some English Bibles trans-
late it "singing," it means "to speak."

People often say, "I wish I could sing like
an angel." Perhaps angels are saying, "I wish I
could sing like a saint." I suspect that there are

---

[3]Ibid., 82–83.

angels who are in our worship services some-
times. I think that they may slip up to some
believers who don't sing the way they should.
Surely, they must nudge that person and say,
"Sing!" What a privilege it is to sing praises to
God!

You're probably still wondering if angels
sing or not. I hope I haven't ruined any of your
Christmas carols. Actually, angels may sing. All
I'm saying is that you never find where they
sing in the Bible. Don't get hung up on this
point. Just be careful the next time you say,
"She sings like an angel." We may get to heaven
and find that angels sing beautifully. If they
do, I will be the first one to apologize. As I
stated earlier, where the Bible speaks, I speak.
Where the Bible is silent, I have to be silent. I
believe that only saints enjoy the privilege of
singing.

FANTASY: All angels are good and obey
   God.
BIBLICAL FACT: Some angels are evil
   and oppose God.

There are only three angels who are named
in the Bible: Michael, Gabriel, and Lucifer.
Michael is the archangel and Gabriel is a special messenger angel.

The other angel named in the Bible is Lucifer. At one time, Lucifer was an angel, even
a cherub. He tried to rebel against God and
was cast out of his position of honor. Now he
is called Satan, the devil. He has many fallen

angels who are called demons or evil spirits. So, in addition to God's holy angels, there are evil, fallen angels. That is why in Matthew 25:41, Jesus said that "hell is prepared for the devil and his angels." You see, angels have a will, and they can choose. Some of them chose to join Lucifer in rebellion against God.

Most people have heard sermons on Satan and demons. I never devote much time to teaching on Satan because he is not worth it. I don't think the devil is worthy of that much of my time. Let's give attention to God and to His holy angels. This book will not discuss Lucifer and his army, but God's good messengers, His angels. We will be focusing on the interaction of God's army with His people.

> FANTASY: Angels must be seen to be real.
> BIBLICAL FACT: Angels are usually invisible; only at times are we enabled to see them.

I would like to see an angel, and you probably would, too. I heard the funny story about a pastor who was studying about angels, and he said, "Lord, I would just like to see an angel. Can you send me one?" Poof! There was an angel in his study.

The angel said, "Here I am. Would you like to take my picture?"

The pastor looked around, pulled out his old camera, and took a picture of the angel. He rushed the film to a shop to be developed.

When he got his pictures and looked at them, he was quite disappointed. The pictures were all dim and blurred. He couldn't see a thing. The moral of that story is that "the spirit was willing, but the flash was weak." Actually, sometimes the spirit (an angel) is probably more willing to be seen than we imagine.

I believe we don't see more angels with our physical eyes because we would be tempted to do what the apostle John did. In the Book of Revelation, we read that he fell down to worship an angel. The angel violently objected, saying, "No, don't you worship me. Worship God only" (Rev. 22:9).

I suspect that if you saw an angel, you would be so transfixed by the vision that you would want to fall down and worship the angel. Angels aren't meant to be worshipped. While we study angels, our devotion must be constantly drawn back to the Lord Jesus Christ and to God the Father, who has blessed us with these angels.

A staff member in our church and his wife, Glen and Dottie Wierick, shared their encounter with an invisible helper.

Angel Encounter
by
Glen and Dottie Wierick

It was the second night of a prayer revival. A sparse crowd was present and the Holy Spirit manifested Himself to my wife,

Dottie, and me in a silent and powerful manner. T.W. Hunt was leading the meeting when all of a sudden he stopped speaking. Nothing but overpowering silence filled the room. Then there was an awesome presence of God that moved through the room. Not everyone felt Him. Several stood and praised God. Some confessed sins. Some sang. Everyone sat in silence. Many were changed that night, others were not.

Dottie and I experienced God anew in our lives that night. Later we found that He was preparing us for difficult times; times that I wouldn't have missed for the world.

After praying for peace of mind at the breakfast table the next morning, my wife Dottie and I discussed books we had been reading about angels. I was especially interested in that verse in Hebrews 13:2 where we are urged to entertain strangers "whereby some have entertained angels unaware." In the course of our conversation I said that I would like to meet an angel personally. Dottie and I prayed for peace of mind and I went on to the office.

I arrived at the receptionist's desk at the church where I, formerly, was on staff, checked my mail and phone calls, and headed down the hall to my office. On the way I met a black shoeshine man dressed in blue jeans, a torn, black leather jacket, and tattered tennis

*shoes. He asked me if I would like a shoe
shine. I looked at my rather dull black shoes
and said, "Why not?"*

*We went into my office, closed the door,
and sat down. I took off my shoes and handed
them to him. He shined my shoes and we
talked for about an hour. I soon realized that
he was different from what I envisioned a
black shoeshine man would be. At first we
talked of simple things—the beauty of East
Texas flowers in the spring, how simple life
should be, relationships with other people. The
conversation grew deeper and deeper beyond
most human conversations which touch only
surface subjects. His perception of spiritual
things was more than mere words could express. It was as though inner souls were communicating. As we talked, I realized that I
was relieved of the stress that I carried to the
office earlier that morning.*

*At one point I paused and asked, "Are you
an angel?"*

*Without the slightest expression of sur-
prise, he responded, "God uses many people
to communicate His message."*

*He finished my shoes and I gave him more
than the two dollar charge he set, for he looked
as if he could use the money. I asked him
where he was going next.*

"Dallas," he said.

I asked him how he would get there.

"Hitchhike, I suppose."

In my staff position with the church, I dealt with transients who came to the church seeking food, housing, and transportation. I had an arrangement with the bus company whereby I would write a brief letter of approval, requesting transportation for a transient to a certain destination. I would include the person's name and destination and indicate approval for the charges to be made to the church's account.

Typing the letter, I asked, "What is your name?"

"Willie Peace," he responded.

"How do you spell your last name?" I said.

"P-E-A-C-E" he replied.

I handed him the finished letter, prayed with him, and he was gone. An exciting euphoria of "peace of mind" strangely encompassed me.

I grabbed my calendar and hurried on to the staff meeting. When everyone had gathered around the huge table, I asked, "Did anybody see the black shoeshine man in the hall a moment ago?"

Silence filled the room. No one had seen Willie Peace but me!

In my heart I knew that God had answered our prayer and request that morning. Hebrews 13:2 had become a physical reality in my life. I did indeed "entertain angels unaware."

Limited Perception

Do you know why you can't see angels? Let's face it. Our human perception is not all that highly developed, even when compared to the perception of God's other creatures. For instance, most of us don't smell very well. (I mean that our olfactory sense is not as highly developed as that of other animals.) If you were a dog in a room full of people, you would be able to detect each person's individual odor. Aren't you glad you're not a dog? Thankfully, our perception is not as sensitive as a dog's when it comes to smelling.

Our sensory perception is not as refined as that of other creatures when it comes to hearing. Some animals can hear ultrasound that is so high-pitched that it is beyond our auditory range. Again, a dog's ears can pick up the sound of a high-frequency "silent whistle." There are other animals that can hear infrasound. These are low, sonic waves that we can't detect. Elephants and whales hear these sounds that are too low for human hearing. Our hearing range is actually limited to a narrow band.

The same is true of our vision. Some of God's creatures can see much better than we can, even with our glasses. A hawk or an eagle can detect, from a great altitude, the movement of a rat in tall grass. Even a housefly with over a hundred eyes, is able to detect things differently than we can. The fact that we can't see everything with our eyes is not our fault.

We were created with a limited sense of perception.

Chapter 6 of 2 Kings tells a story that all of us need to learn if we hope to ever see an angel. It is the story of the prophet Elisha who went out to fight against the army of the Syrians. There were only two good guys—Elisha and his servant. Across the valley was an entire army of Syrian soldiers arrayed against them.

The servant was mortified. He asked, "What are we going to do, master?"

Elisha replied, "They that be with us are more than they that be with them" (2 Kings 6:16).

I can imagine that the dumbfounded servant said, "What? There are only two of us! And look at all the Syrians, there must be hundreds and thousands of them. What are you talking about?"

Elisha prayed a prayer, "God, open the eyes of my servant" (2 Kings 6:17).

The Bible says the servant's eyes were opened and that he saw that the mountains were full of flaming chariots, with horses and soldiers. An army of angelic warriors was there to support them. They had been there all along; the servant just didn't see them. In answer to his prayer, God granted Elisha's servant the ability to see what was already there. God sometimes allows us to see angels, too.

Be careful that you don't develop angelic paranoia. I believe that if God would open our spiritual eyes, we would be amazed at the an-

gels surrounding us. For instance, I suspect
there are hundreds of angels who gather with
believers each week when they assemble to
worship. Look around next Sunday and ask
God to open your eyes.

We read in Psalm 91:11–12, "For he will
command his angels concerning you to guard
you in all your ways; they will lift you up in
their hands, so that you will not strike your
foot against a stone." God promises to send
His angels to help you, to protect you, and
sometimes to deliver messages, but the angels
usually are imperceptible helpers hidden from
our view. Only rarely does He allow us to visu-
ally perceive these angelic helpers. The following encounter portrays this truth.

Angel Encounter
by
Doug Knapp
(Missionary to Tanzania)

*There was an African man named Abali
who was a carpenter. He wanted to start
churches, so the Foreign Mission Board gave
him a little motorcycle to use in his travels.
Abali had the desire to minister to a church
that was on the other side of a steep, desolate
mountain.*

*On that mountain there was a rugged trail
that followed a ledge around the mountain.
The trail practically went straight up and
down. As he was riding his motorcycle he*

came to a place where the ledge had fallen, and there was a makeshift bridge made of two logs and some boards tied to them.

Abali climbed off his motorcycle and cautiously pushed it across this precarious bridge. Just as he was reaching the other side, the boards beneath his feet collapsed and he fell through. He had his legs and one arm holding on to a log and the other arm holding the motorcycle to keep it from falling. Abali could not pull himself up without letting go of the motorcycle and losing his only means of transportation.

He cried out helplessly, "God, Help me!"

No sooner had the words left his mouth than an old African man appeared carrying a basket. He asked Abali in his native tribal tongue, "What can I do to help you?"

Abali told him to take the motorcycle and push it on across. The man walked around him, set his basket down, and pushed the motorcycle across. Abali pulled himself up, carefully walked on across, and looked up to thank the man, but he had disappeared.

Abali got on his motorcycle, for he knew he could overtake the man since he was on foot, but he never saw him again. As Abali thought about it, he realized that the man must have been an angel. For what would an old man have been doing on foot so far from any village? How would the man have known his tribal tongue? How would the man have known that

Abali was from that specific tribe? And how could he have disappeared so quickly? An angel is the only explanation.

Face the Facts

Angels exist, but most people embrace fantastic fantasies about them. In order to appreciate their existence and appreciate their help, you must choose to believe what the Bible says about angels. As you open your mind to the truth about angels, God can more easily open your eyes to see the ministry of angels around you.

Section II
Jesus: The Master of Angels

Angels are God's secret agents, His supernatural helpers who are sent to assist us and to deliver messages. Although this study emphasizes the truth about angels, our focus should always be on the Lord Jesus Christ. Many people are interested in the topic of angels because they are fascinated with supernatural beings. In this book, you will read of numerous accounts from individuals who believe that they have had encounters with angels. As remarkable as each experience is, we must remember to keep our eyes firmly focused on the Lord Jesus Christ, who has provided us with these angelic helpers.

When you think about angels, I hope that you use your spiritual peripheral vision. Sometimes when you look directly at a star at night, you cannot see it; but when you look to the side you get a clearer picture of that star. Our focus should be on Jesus. We should be looking unto Jesus, the Author and Finisher of our faith. We can keep Jesus in view and be aware of the presence of God's ministering spirits. All of the New Testament, from Matthew through Revelation, shows how angels interfaced with the life and ministry of the Lord Jesus Christ.

Chapter 3

Angels at the Birth and Temptation of Jesus

We read in Matthew 1:18–21,

> This is how the birth of Jesus Christ came about: His mother Mary pledged to be married to Joseph, but before they came together, she was found to be with child through the Holy Spirit. Because Joseph her husband was a righteous man and did not want to expose her to public disgrace, he had in mind to divorce her quietly.
>
> But after he had considered this, an angel of the Lord appeared to him in a dream and said, "Joseph son of David, do not be afraid to take Mary home as your wife, because what is conceived in her is from the Holy Spirit. She will give birth to a son, and you are to give him the name Jesus, because he will save his people from their sins."

As we study the Scriptures, we find that angels have an interesting ministry in announc-

ing the birth of babies. The first time we en-
counter angels in the Bible is in the Book of
Genesis when an angel appeared to Hagar and
informed her that she was going to give birth
(Gen. 16:7–11). Angels came to Abraham and
Sarah and told them they were to have a baby
(Gen. 18:10). It was an angel who appeared to
Moroah, the father of Samson, and told him
and his wife they would be parents of a son
(Judg. 13:3). This angel even prescribed a diet
for the mother of Samson to eat during her
pregnancy, so I call it a dietician angel. It could
be that some of these angels are "obstetric
angels" because they are so interested in the
birth of babies. An angel appeared to Zachariah,
the father of John the Baptist, to announce the
birth of that child.

In the most familiar birth announcements,
angels came to Mary and to Joseph and announced that Jesus Christ was going to be born.

Luke recorded that the angel Gabriel told
Mary,

> "You will be with child and give birth to
> a son, and you are to give him the name
> Jesus. He will be great and will be called
> the Son of the Most High. The Lord God
> will give him the throne of his father
> David, and he will reign over the house
> of Jacob forever; his kingdom will never
> end."

> "How will this be," Mary asked the an-
> gel, "since I am a virgin?"

> The angel answered, "The Holy Spirit
> will come upon you, and the power of
> the Most High will overshadow you. So
> the holy one to be born will be called the
> Son of God." (Luke 1:31–35)

When Joseph discovered that Mary, his espoused wife, was pregnant, he had a choice of legal options. One option was to follow a prescribed ceremony to publicly shame her. Another possibility was to have her publicly stoned. That stoning was an option is verified later in the New Testament when the woman caught in adultery was brought before Jesus to be stoned.

Joseph, however, decided that he would do neither of those things. Rather, he would just put her away quietly. Then an angel came and said, "Joseph son of David, do not be afraid to take Mary home as your wife, because what is conceived in her is from the Holy Spirit. She will give birth to a son, and you are to give him the name Jesus, because he will save his people from their sins" (Matt. 1:20–21).

The virgin birth of Jesus Christ is not some incidental doctrine of our faith, but is absolutely essential to belief in the deity of Jesus Christ.

If you want to use an interesting little riddle as a tool to open up a witnessing conversation, say to someone, "Who was the only baby born who was older than his mother and the same age as his daddy?" Do you know the answer? Jesus Christ. He was older than His mother.

What do you mean? Jesus said, "Before Abraham was, I Am" (John 8:58). Jesus Christ has always existed in the form of God, the Son. He was the same age of His father because His father was God Almighty.

When you look at a nativity scene and see Mary and Joseph portrayed there, remember that Mary was the mother of Jesus, but Joseph was not the father of Jesus. He took care of Jesus, but God was the father of the Lord Jesus Christ. So, the first place that we see angels operating in the life of Jesus was when they announced His birth.

Angels Assisted Christ During His Temptation

Matthew 4:1 declares: "Then Jesus was led by the Spirit into the desert to be tempted by the devil. After fasting forty days and forty nights, he was hungry. The tempter came to him and said, 'If you are the Son of God, tell these stones to become bread.' " Again, the devil challenged, "If you are the Son of God, cast yourself off of the pinnacle of the temple" (see Matt. 4:5–10). Then Satan misquoted Psalm 91 about the angels lifting Him up. He said, "If you are the Son of God, bow down and worship me and all these kingdoms will be yours." Three times the devil tempted Him, and three times Jesus overcame the temptation.

The easy way Jesus resisted temptation is the same way we resist temptation. Three times

Jesus took the sword of the Word of God and said, "It is written." "It is written." "It is written." And, he quoted Scripture. The best way for you and me to overcome temptation is to have the Word of God hidden in our hearts. We don't memorize Scripture so that we can pass a discipleship course. We memorize Scripture so we can stay clean before the Lord. The Bible says, "Thy word have I hid in my heart that I might not sin against thee" (Ps. 119:11, KJV).

After Jesus completed His temptation and was victorious, something else happened. There is more in Matthew 4:11. Sometimes we forget this part of the experience. "Then the devil left him, and angels came and attended him." The *King James Bible* says they ministered unto him. The word *ministered* or *attended* is the Greek word *diakoneo*, from which we get our word *deacon*.

The role of a deacon is to minister, to care for. I thank God for all the deacons who understand that their biblical goal is one of service and ministry. Angels were there assisting Jesus at this time of temptation. That word *ministering* or *attending* could mean that they fed Him a meal. Jesus was hungry. He had been without food for forty days and forty nights. A gourmet angel fed Elijah under a juniper tree (1 Kings 19:5–8). Perhaps, it could be that the angels ministered to Jesus in that way.

When you think of the temptation of Jesus, you usually think only of this temptation. The

Scripture says He was tempted in all points as we are. Yet, He never sinned. For instance, the other great temptation He faced was at the end of His ministry when He came into the Garden of Gethsemane, and the cross was looming large in front of Him. He was tempted to take the easy way out. He said, "Father, take this cup from me. Nevertheless, not my will but yours be done" (Matt. 26:39).

The Bible says He faced that temptation, overcame it, and committed Himself to the cross. Then the Scripture says that an angel came and ministered to Him after He resisted that temptation. His ministry is bracketed by two times of intense temptation. Each time angels came and helped Him through it. Sometimes when you hear angel stories, you think they are something supernatural and amazing. Sometimes they are very common, ordinary experiences.

One lady wrote to me that she has two sons who are very active little boys. She related that one Sunday morning she was trying to get them ready for Sunday school. When she got one boy cleaned up and dressed, she set him to the side and started working on the second one to get him dressed for church.

While she was dressing the second one, the first one got up under the bathroom sink. Somehow, he got in all the grease on the pipes underneath the sink and got wet and dirty. She turned back to redress him. While she was redressing the first one, the second one went outside and jumped in the dirt. She said that she finally got both of them in front of her, and she was about ready to lose her temper. She was tempted to scream and execute judgment on them at that moment, but she said, "Get thee behind me, Satan." She said that once she resisted the temptation to lose her temper, it was as if she could feel somebody putting hands on her arms from behind and saying, "Settle down. Calm down. Take it easy."

I think that sometimes when we resist temptation, the angels do for us what they did for the Lord Jesus Christ: they help us.

Chapter 4

Jesus Taught about Angels

In the midst of so much modern confusion about angels, it is wise for us to study carefully the truth that Jesus conveyed about angels. When you study the four gospel accounts, it is clear that Jesus did not intend to establish an exhaustive treatise about angels. Instead, He gives us brief glimpses into the nature and activity of these ministering spirits. These teachings can be categorized into ten distinctive truths.

(1) Jesus Taught about the Role of Angels at the End of the World

The return of Jesus to planet earth is taught throughout the New Testament. Christian groups may disagree about the details of His return, but anyone who reads Scripture cannot deny the fact of His Second Coming.

Jesus says in Matthew 13:41–42: "The Son of Man will send out his angels, and they will weed out of the kingdom everything that causes sin and all who do evil. They will throw them into the fiery furnace, where there will be weeping and gnashing of teeth."

Although angels will accompany Jesus at His return, it is obvious that they don't know when this event will occur. He taught, "No one knows about that day or hour, not even the angels in heaven, nor the Son, but only the Father" (Matt. 24:36). Today there are many self-proclaimed prophets who claim to know more than the angels (or even the Son) because they are predicting when Jesus will return.

Whenever I read or hear of someone who has predicted the date of Christ's return, I know immediately that he is wrong—Jesus made it clear that even the angels don't know the day or the hour. As one of my friends likes to say, "When it comes to the Second Coming, I'm not the scheduling committee, I'm on the welcoming committee!"

(2) Jesus Taught that Children Have Angels Who Are Interested in Their Care

In Matthew 18:10, He said, "See that you do not look down on one of these little ones. For I tell you that their angels in heaven always see the face of my Father in heaven." This verse has been greatly misunderstood. Many have taken this as the proof text to teach that there is a "guardian angel" assigned to every child, and perhaps to every Christian, regardless of age. As will be discussed later, angels do guard us; however, if you try to find Scripture to substantiate the teaching that one particular angel stays with us all of our lives, you'll be disappointed. The Bible doesn't teach that.

The key to understanding this teaching of Jesus is to simply notice where He says these angels are. Are they on earth, with these children constantly? That's not at all what He says. He says that these angels are in heaven, looking into the face of the Father.

Angels are not omnipresent—they can't be both in heaven and on earth simultaneously. It may be that when Jesus says "their angels," He could be referring to multiple angels who shuttle between heaven and earth and get their direction from the Father.

(3) Jesus Taught that Angels Don't Marry

In Mark 12, Jesus is asked a loaded question by a man who doesn't believe in life after death. It was a sarcastic question about a woman who had been married seven times. The Sadducee finished his question with a comical flair: "At the resurrection whose wife will she be, since the seven were married to her?" (Mark 12:23). Instead of being insulted by this far-fetched riddle, Jesus uses it as an opportunity to teach us something about our resurrection condition and about angels.

Jesus replied to the man, "When the dead rise, they will neither marry nor be given in

marriage; they will be like the angels in heaven"
(Mark 12:25). Before you can understand the
truth of this amazing statement, you must first
comprehend what Jesus is not saying. First, He
isn't saying that we become angels when we
die—He says we are like angels in respect to
new relationships. Second, Jesus is not saying
that we won't maintain the knowledge of our
spouses when we get to heaven. He is simply
saying that there will be no new marriages—no
wedding bells for human weddings in heaven.

In this statement, our Lord is giving us keen
insight into the nature of angels. Angels do not
marry. In fact, we never read in the Bible of
female angels. Angels always appear as men.
God created the first woman, Eve, as a neces-
sary companion and helper to Adam. Angels
do not share the same need for companion-
ship and marriage.

Some believe that this teaches that angels
are sexless or without gender. That may be
stretching the truth, because in Genesis 19, two
angels entered Sodom and the wicked men of
Sodom wanted to have sex with them. The Bible
doesn't say if this was even a possibility, but at
least it appeared to those Sodomites that it was
possible.

Another fascinating Scripture related to this
is Genesis 6:1–4. This speaks of "sons of God"
who had sexual relations with women before
the flood. The result was a race of giants called
"Nephilim." Some commentators believe these
were angels and tie this event with Jude 6, which
speaks of angels who did not "keep their posi-

tion" and are chained in darkness for future judgment. Don't study these Scriptures unless you want to spend a lot of time scratching your head.

This gets really confusing, and it's impossible to make a dogmatic conclusion from these Scriptures. However, we are safe to insist that angels do not marry one another. Some husbands today may insist that "I married an angel," but an angel himself will never make that claim. You'll never receive an invitation to an "angel wedding."

(4) Jesus Taught that Angels Do Not Die

You'll never receive an invitation to attend an "angel funeral" either. You'll never read an angel obituary. Except for the generation of Christians alive when Jesus returns, we will all die. "Man is destined to die once, and after that to face judgment" (Heb. 9:27). However, once a Christian has died and faced God's judgment, he won't ever die again (a nonbeliever will suffer the "second death" according to Revelation 20:14).

In teaching this truth, Jesus also taught us something about angels: "and they can no longer die; for they are like the angels" (Luke 20:36). Search the Scriptures to see if you can discover the death of an angel. It's not there. Physical death in a person can be caused by sickness, injury, or simply old age. The Bible never speaks of an angel getting sick or injured. We never read of a "baby angel" or a "geriatric angel." It seems as if Jesus is teaching that angels never age or die—they are eternal spiritual beings. It's wonderful to realize that one day we will be like the angels in this respect.

(5) Jesus Taught that the Devil Has Angels to Assist Him

Some people often ask why God ever created a hell. Jesus gives the answer and at the same moment teaches us something about angels. He said, "Depart from me, you who are cursed, into the eternal fire prepared for the devil and his angels" (Matt. 25:41). God never desired for hell to be inhabited by human beings—it was for Satan and the fallen angels. However, whenever a person rejects God's love and His free gift of eternal life, he is choosing his own hellish destiny for eternity.

Who are the devil's angels? They are sometimes called demons, or evil spirits. Just as angels are ministering spirits, the devil has his assistants who are malevolent spirits. Some commentators believe that when Lucifer rebelled against God, many angels chose to join him. Some interpret Revelation 12:4 to mean that fully one-third of the angels were swept from heaven with Lucifer.

Remember, Satan is only a fallen angel himself. He is not omnipresent. Unlike God, Satan cannot be everywhere at once. However, he has an organized, demonized army of fallen angels to assist him in his devilish strategy.

(6) Jesus Taught that Angels Could Have Rescued Him from the Cross

On the night before Jesus was crucified, He was arrested in the Garden of Gethsemane. Peter tried to defend Jesus by drawing his sword. Jesus rebuked him and then He revealed that an angelic army was available to Him. He said, "Put your sword back in its place, for all who draw the sword will die by the sword. Do you think I cannot call on my Father, and he will at once put at my disposal more than twelve legions of angels?" (Matt. 26:52–53).

I am in awe at the power and impact of that statement. A legion usually described six thousand soldiers. Throughout the entire ordeal of the trial, torture, and crucifixion of Jesus, He could have simply asked the Father and seventy-two thousand angels would have been instantly dispatched for His aid.

Try to imagine yourself as an angel during those moments in which God the Son was being brutally victimized by sinful man. It must have been agonizing for the angels to watch helplessly as man, the creature, abused God the Creator. I can imagine that the angel army was poised on the ramparts of heaven with its swords drawn. I think that they must have wanted the Father to give them the Divine "go ahead" so they could have rescued their Lord.

Why didn't Jesus call for them? He answers that by what He says next to Simon Peter: "But how then would the Scriptures be fulfilled that say it must happen in this way?" (Matt. 26:54). Jesus was so conscious of fulfilling God's Word that He refused to call for help. He demonstrated such stubborn love for us, that He suffered silently when help was only a prayer away. Hallelujah, what a Saviour!

(7) Jesus Taught that There Is Joy in the Presence of Angels when a Person Repents

In Luke 15, Jesus tells three consecutive stories about something that is lost, then is found. He is really teaching us what God is like. He first tells of a shepherd who leaves his sheep to search for one lost lamb. This speaks of God's searching love. Next, He tells of a woman who loses ten coins and turns her house upside down to find them. She doesn't give up until they are all found. This speaks of God's stubborn love. Jesus completes the trilogy by telling of a father whose son leaves and then returns. This speaks of God's suffering love.

In each of these stories, there is a scene of joy when the sheep, the silver, and the son are found. Jesus says, "In the same way, I tell you, there is rejoicing in the presence of the angels of God over one sinner who repents" (Luke 15:10). I've often heard this verse slightly misquoted. Some people say "the angels rejoice over one sinner who repents." While that may be true, that's not what Jesus said. Look at it again. He said there is joy "in the presence of angels" when one sinner repents. Does the joy come from the angels themselves or from the One in whose presence they are?

The language seems to indicate that Someone else is rejoicing and the angels witness and benefit from the rejoicing. When you understand this, it is a bonus blessing. When you became a Christian, it made God joyous. He rejoiced over your return to Him (just like the father of the prodigal son). The angels (like the servants) were part of the feast and celebration that followed salvation. The thing that makes heaven happy certainly ought to make us happy as well. Do you get excited when a person comes to Christ? Heaven does!

(8) Jesus Taught that Angels Escort Our Souls to Paradise

In Luke 16, Jesus tells another fascinating truth about angels. He relates the story of an unnamed rich man and a righteous beggar named Lazarus. In Luke 16:22, He said, "The time came when the beggar died and the angels carried him to Abraham's side."

This beautiful truth will be explored in a later chapter. At this point, it's just comforting to know that God sends his "escort angels" to

insure that our souls are seen safely into heaven
when we die. That's another reason why a Christian never has to fear death.

(9) Jesus Taught that Angels
Travel Back and Forth to Heaven

In the first chapter of John's Gospel, Jesus
surprises Nathanael by revealing his location
and by peering into his character. When
Nathanael responds with amazement, Jesus re-
plies, "You believe because I told you I saw you
under the fig tree. You shall see greater things
than that. I tell you the truth, you shall see
heaven open, and the angels of God ascending
and descending on the Son of Man" (John 1:50–
51).

If your spiritual eyes were suddenly opened,
I believe you would see a steady stream of angels
traveling to and from heaven. It seems that
some angels are "on active duty" on earth at
times, and then are relieved by other angels, at
which time they get to return to heaven for a
little "R and R" (revelation and rejoicing).

Jacob observed the same vision in a dream
described in Genesis 32. He saw a stairway into
heaven with angels ascending and descending.
As children, we used to sing "we are climbing
Jacob's ladder." Actually, you can't get into
heaven by climbing Jacob's ladder—only Jesus
can get you into heaven. Jacob's ladder is
marked "angels only."

(10) Jesus Taught that Angels Witness Our Confession of Jesus

In Luke 12:8–9, Jesus said, "I tell you, whoever acknowledges me before men, the Son of Man will also acknowledge him before the angels of God. But he who disowns me before men will be disowned before the angels of God." This truth contains both an encouragement and a warning. Whenever we publicly confess that Jesus is our Lord, He is faithful to claim us as His child before the angels. However, if we refuse to accept Him as our Lord, He will disown us before the angels.

I think that is what Jesus is doing in Matthew 7:23 when He utters the most fearful words that an unregenerate church member will ever hear: "Then I will tell them plainly, 'I never knew you. Away from me, you evildoers!' "

It is impossible to remain a "closet Christian." Jesus requires that we publicly acknowledge Him before our peers. When it comes to confessing Jesus, silence is not golden—it is yellow. Have you confessed Jesus as your personal Lord? If you have, the angels will hear about it from Jesus.

In these ten statements we discover that Jesus believed in angels and He taught us of the wonderful ministry they provide. Because Jesus interacted with angels, we shouldn't be afraid to welcome their ministry in our lives.

Angels at the Death and Resurrection of Jesus

We have already noted that twelve legions of angels were available for Jesus to call during His torture and crucifixion (Matt. 26:52). The fact that He did not summon these angels is a testimony to His great love for us.

After Jesus died, He was buried in a tomb provided by Joseph of Arimathea. What happened three days later is amazing. The setting in Matthew 28:1–7 describes the first Sunday morning.

> After the Sabbath, at dawn on the first day of the week, Mary Magdalene and the other Mary went to look at the tomb.

> There was a violent earthquake, for an angel of the Lord came down from heaven and, going to the tomb, rolled back the stone and sat on it. His appearance was like lightning, and his clothes were white as snow.

Have you ever wondered why in artistic depictions, angels are often seen with halos? A halo is descriptive of the kind of glory, the brightness that seems to be representative of their character. The angel's clothes were white as snow, whiter than any modern detergent could ever get them.

> The guards were so afraid of him that they shook and became like dead men. The angel said to the women, "Do not be afraid, for I know that you are looking for Jesus, who was crucified. He is not here; he is risen, just as he said. Come and see the place where he lay. Then go quickly and tell his disciples: 'He has risen from the dead and is going ahead of you into Galilee. There you will see him.' Now I have told you."

Isn't it interesting to see how all through the life and ministry of Jesus, angels were there? Even at the tomb of the Lord Jesus there was an angel who came down. The reason the stone was rolled away was not for Jesus to walk out. He didn't need an exit cleared. The stone was moved so that we could look into the tomb and see that it was empty. I can imagine that the big strong angel came down there, took that stone, tossed it aside, sat on top of it, crossed his legs, and waited for the women to come. The Bible said those strong, brave Roman soldiers were so afraid that they shook, trembled, and became like dead men. The angels pronounced the first Easter message, "He is not here. He is risen!"

Angels and the Second Coming

Jesus died, was buried, and after three days and three nights, He was restored to life. For forty days He remained on the earth, appearing to over five hundred people, but at the end of that forty-day period, he ascended back into heaven. Observe what the angels said when He ascended back into heaven. In Acts 1:10–11, we are told,

> They were looking intently up into the sky as he was going, when suddenly two men dressed in white stood beside them. "Men of Galilee," they said, "why do you stand here looking into the sky? This same Jesus, who has been taken from you into heaven, will come back in the same way you have seen him go into heaven."

The disciples stood there and watched Jesus ascend into the sky. I can imagine they looked at him for as long as they could, like people watching a space shuttle, trying to keep their eyes on it until it becomes a tiny speck in the sky. Finally, their attention was drawn away by these two angels who made the startling announcement that Jesus was going to return.

Angels Will Accompany Him at His Second Coming

All Christians will not agree on all the details of the Second Coming of Jesus Christ, but we do know that He is going to return and that His angels are coming with Him.

In Matthew 24:30–31, Jesus had this to say about His Second Coming.

> At that time the sign of the Son of Man will appear in the sky, and all the nations of the earth will mourn. They will see the Son of Man coming on the clouds of the sky, with power and great glory. And he will send his angels with a loud trumpet call, and they will gather his elect from the four winds, from one end of the heavens to the other.

Jesus Himself said, "When I come back in my power and glory I am going to send my angels and they are going to be the ones who will gather to me, all those who are mine, who are the elect" (Matt. 24:31). They will come with Him.

Angels Will Accomplish His Judgment

If you want to learn about angels, consult the Book of Revelation where angels are mentioned more than seventy times. This is more than in any other single book in the Bible.

In Matthew 13:24–30, 36–43, Jesus tells the story of the wheat and the tares.

> Jesus told them another parable: "The kingdom of heaven is like a man who sowed good seed in his field. But while everyone was sleeping, his enemy came and sowed weeds among the wheat, and went away. When the wheat sprouted and formed heads, then the weeds also appeared.
>
> "The owner's servants came to him an said, 'Sir, didn't you sow good seed in your field? Where then did the weeds come from?'
>
> " 'An enemy did this,' he replied.
>
> "The servants asked him, 'Do you want us to go and pull them up?'
>
> " 'No,' he answered, 'because while you are pulling the weeds, you may root up the wheat with them. Let both grow together until the harvest. At that time I will tell the harvesters: First collect the weeds and tie them in bundles to be burned; then gather the wheat and bring it into my barn.' "
>
> Then he left the crowd and went into the house. His disciples came to him and said, "Explain to us the parable of the weeds in the field."

He answered, "The one who sowed the good seed is the Son of Man. The field is the world, and the good seed stands for the sons of the kingdom. The weeds are the sons of the evil one, and the enemy who sows them is the devil. The harvest is the end of the age, and the harvesters are angels.

"As the weeds are pulled up and burned in the fire, so it will be at the end of the age. The Son of Man will send out his angels, and they will weed out of his kingdom everything that causes sin and all who do evil. They will throw them into the fiery furnace, where there will be weeping and gnashing of teeth. Then the righteous will shine like the sun in the kingdom of their Father. He who has ears, let him hear."

The judge is the Lord Jesus Christ, but you might say that His bailiffs, His policemen, are His angels. He will send them forth to execute His judgment. All the unrighteous will be gathered up by the angels and judgment will come upon their lives. God is not willing that any should perish, but that all should come to repentance.

In Matthew 25, Jesus says hell was prepared for the devil and his angels. God didn't prepare hell for you. He wants everyone to be saved. I hope that you have trusted the Lord Jesus Christ with your heart so that when the future judgment comes, you will not be in that number who will have judgment executed upon them.

Not only will the angels execute judgment upon the righteous, but an angel will be the one who executes judgment upon the fallen angel, Satan himself. A whole army of angels is not needed—not a battalion, not a legion, but one single angel will accomplish the overthrow of Satan.

> And I saw an angel coming down out of heaven, having the key to the Abyss and holding in his hand a great chain. He seized the dragon, that ancient serpent, who is the devil, or Satan, and bound him for a thousand years. He threw him into the Abyss, and locked and sealed it over him, to keep him from deceiving the nations anymore until the thousand years were ended. After that, he must be set free for a short time. (Rev. 20:1–3)

The devil will have a brief furlough from his prison, but then he will be cast back in for eternity. I like the way it teaches that the angel is going to come with a chain, and he is going to wrap up Satan, throttle him, put him in the bottom of his pit and shut him up. Don't you look forward to the day when the devil will be shut up forever? God will use His angel to do that.

You ask what all this means. It means that Jesus taught about angels and angels ministered

in the life of Jesus, so we should believe in them.
We need to look for their ministry as we serve
the Lord Jesus. As you learn of God's working in
our lives through His Holy Spirit and through
His ministering spirits, may your desire be to obey
Him and to serve Him.

Section III
The Ministry of Angels

Since angels are "ministering spirits" sent to help us, what is it that they do? This section will explore the various ways that God's wonderful angels minister to the saints.

Chapter 7

Angels Pronounce
God's Message to Us

When a missionary group from our church was in the former Soviet Union during the summer of 1993, we bought some watches from a street vendor. On the band was a figure of a man's face. We tried to ask the vendor who that person was, but we didn't have a translator. The man kept pointing to the sky when we pointed to the face. We wrinkled our brows and asked, "Is that Jesus or God?" We finally discovered that it was a picture of the first Soviet cosmonaut, Yuri Gargaran. He is a hero to the Soviet people.

As you will recall, in 1960, he made history as the first man to go into space. He came back to earth and made his famous statement, "I've been to the heavens and I did not see God." Ten years later, Yuri Gargaran died mysteriously in a plane crash. By the way, that is when he saw God.

It is interesting that years later, some of the Soviet cosmonauts gave a very different report about heaven or space. A December 1990 article in *USA Today* states that six Soviet cosmonauts witnessed the most awe-inspiring spectacle ever encountered in space—a band of glowing angels as big as jumbo jets. What they saw, the space travelers said, were seven giant figures in forms of humans with mist-like halos as in the classic depiction of angels. Their faces were round with cherubic smiles. Twelve days later, the figures returned and were seen by three other Soviet scientists, including female cosmonaut Elana Stepharich. "They were smiling," she said, "as though they shared in a glorious secret."

There is no secret. God's Word and modern testimonies bear the truth that there are angels, God's ministering spirits. Even though we might not always see them, angels exist. God uses His angels for specific purposes. Do you know the ministry of angels?

Simply believing that angels exist is not enough. You won't fully appreciate them until you recognize their purpose. Several years ago, I read an interesting story about the Whamo Toy Company. This company has the patent for the popular Frisbee. Through a charitable trust the company sent five hundred Frisbees to an African orphanage. No explanation was included with the toys.

The president of Whamo Toy Company received an interesting letter from Sister Dominic, who runs the orphanage. She wrote, "Dear Sir, Thank you for the plastic dishes. We eat off them every meal, but an amazing thing has happened. Some of the boys have started tossing them and they fly really well. This may be an idea for your toy company."

She didn't realize that was the actual purpose of the Frisbees! I'm afraid some people are guilty of the same mistake. They believe there are angels; they just don't know the real purpose of angels.

In Psalm 34:7, we read: "The angel of the Lord encamps around those who fear him, and he delivers them." In Psalms 91:9–12, we find:

> If you make the Most High your dwelling—even the Lord, who is my refuge—then no harm will befall you, no disaster will come near your tent. For he will command his angels concerning you to guard you in all your ways; they will lift you up in their hands, so that you will not strike your foot against a stone.

God's angels are ministering spirits, sent forth to minister to those who are heirs of salvation. In the next five chapters, we will examine how they minister to us.

God's Messengers

The basic ministry of angels is to deliver God's messages. The word angel (*angelos*) means "messenger." The same word *angelos* is sometimes used in Scripture to describe a human messenger. I believe that in Revelation 3:14, where the writer speaks about "the angel of the church at Laodicea" (or Sardis or Ephesus), the reference is to the human messenger (pastor) of that church.

The Hebrew word for angel is *malachi* (just like the prophet Malachi), which also means "messenger." There are many examples in the Bible where angels function as God's "messenger boys."

In Acts 8:26, we read that God sent an angel to deliver a message to Philip. "Now an angel of the Lord said to Philip, 'Go south to the road—the desert road—that goes down from Jerusalem to Gaza.'" God used this angel to arrange a divine rendezvous between a seeker and a witness. As a result, the Ethiopian eunuch accepted Christ and was baptized.

There is a very important point that we must understand. Have you ever wondered why God didn't just send the angel to preach to the Ethiopian? Nowhere in the Bible do angels ever deliver evangelistic messages to lost people. Some Christians wish that God had arranged it so that they wouldn't have to share their faith. It would be simpler if we could just become Christians, get our ticket to heaven, and not worry about talking to anybody else about Jesus. Some would prefer that God send His angels on Tuesday night or Wednesday night visitation, but that's not His plan. God sends angels to deliver messages to His own children, but He gives us both the privilege and the responsibility of delivering the message of salvation to those who are lost.

I suspect the reason angels never deliver a message about salvation is because they don't comprehend what salvation is. They have never been lost; thus they have never been saved. In 1 Peter 1:12, Peter is discussing salvation. He writes, "Even angels long to look into these things." Angels do not understand grace, faith, or regeneration. I was once lost; now I'm saved. Angels don't understand that experience, so they haven't been given the job of communicating the gospel message. Only we have that message, and we have that job.

So, what message do angels deliver to us? In a nutshell—any message that God gives them! Like a faithful postal employee, they merely deliver the message, they aren't responsible for its content.

Later, in Section V, we will examine in detail the Bible's most common messages that angels deliver to God's children.

Chapter 8

Angels Provide for Our Needs

As I teach about angels, God's ministering spirits, I'm often asked, "What is the difference between angels, God's ministering spirits, and the Holy Spirit? Why doesn't God just do everything through the Holy Spirit?" I don't claim to understand all the mysteries of the Scriptures. There are certain unfathomable truths about the person of God and the reality of angels that we can never figure out. The Bible teaches that the Holy Spirit comes to live inside every Christian. Angels never live inside a person.

Jesus said of the Holy Spirit, "And I will ask the Father, and he will give you another Counselor to be with you forever—the Spirit of truth. The world cannot accept him, because it neither sees him nor knows him. But you know him, for he lives with you and will be in you" (John 14:16–17).

The Holy Spirit attends to us spiritually, whereas God's angels have been given the unique authority to minister to us physically.

Here's an example. In 1 Kings 19:5, we read this about Elijah, "Then he lay down under the tree and fell asleep. All at once an angel touched him and said, 'Get up and eat.'"

Do you remember that story? Elijah, who was physically exhausted, emotionally drained, and spiritually depleted, was sitting under a tree, wanting to die. He said, "I don't want to live any more" (1 Kings 19:4). God sent an angel to minister to his physical needs. Elijah went to sleep and the angel came and poked Elijah in the ribs. We'll learn later that one of the common jobs of angels is to wake people up.

The Bible never says the Holy Spirit can actually touch a person physically, but angels can. So, this angel touched Elijah in the side and said, "Get up and eat" (1 Kings 18:7). The Bible says the food he prepared was a cake. What kind of cake? Obviously, angel food cake!

In Psalms 78:25, we read, "Men ate the bread of angels; he sent them all the food they could eat." This is referring to the manna that God provided each day for the children of Israel in the wilderness. There is something about the nature and ministry of angels that demonstrates that they are able to attend to our physical needs, even in terms of providing food.

Not long ago I talked with a lady, a very well-respected widow who is not unstable—emotionally or spiritually. She shared with me that after the death of her husband, she had a hard time getting over the grief of that event. She said it seemed as if she couldn't stop crying. She said it seemed as if she couldn't stop crying. She had never realized just how big, cold, and empty a bed could be until her husband died.

One night she was in bed, lying on her side. She was crying and praying, saying, "Oh God, when will it end? When will the pain end?" She said, at that moment, she felt arms wrap around and embrace her from behind. She added that she was afraid to look, but those arms were as real as any arms she had ever felt. She went to sleep and slept peacefully that night, which was the beginning of her peace and victory over that time of grief. She told me that she believes it was an angel of God sent to help her, even giving her physical comfort at that time.

In Genesis 32:24, we read about the night when Jacob wrestled all night with a being who is called a man, but who is obviously an angel. So angels can indeed touch us.

Marsha Head's experience with an angel proves this point.

Angel Encounter
by
Marsha Head

As I write down for the first time an angel experience I had thirty-six years ago as a young girl, I ask that the "words of my mouth and the meditations of my heart be acceptable in thy sight, Oh, Lord, my strength and my redeemer."

Many times since that bright summer day

time my mind goes rushing back to that safe harbor to which my angel took me as I was drowning in the waters of a church camp lake. Truly, the peace and strength that angel brought me in the long ago has been a life-long influence for good to me and our family.

During the summer of my fifteenth year, the Presbyterian Youth Choir of Houston, Texas, was making plans to go to Montreat, North Carolina for a choir workshop.

My mom was amazed that I was planning to go, even amazed that I sang in choir at all since I couldn't and still can't, "carry a tune in a bucket." But, I believe because of God's purpose and my destiny to receive God's love, I was included in the trip.

I had grown up in the neighborhood Presbyterian Church, and I loved all the activities and the security of being a part of what was happening. I considered myself a Christian because of my training and regular church attendance.

After growing up in Houston with flat, open land all around me, the beauty of the mountains of North Carolina was breathtaking. The isolation of the camp gave us young people a feeling of total freedom and release from the pressures of city life.

In the afternoons following our morning activities, we were allowed to swim in the camp lake. The lake was about five or six acres in size and its calm, glassy surface reflected the mountains and sky, presenting a gorgeous picture of God's gift to us. It was a totally natural setting and to a city girl accustomed to traffic, flashing lights and the dangers of the Houston area, it was as close to heaven as I had been.

Each day I had become more daring in my swimming ventures into the cold, deep waters. I had never been a good swimmer and my mom, brother, and I had previously had a very close call with the undertow at Galveston Beach. My Dad had pulled us out of a very deep, swiftly moving wave that had swept the ocean floor out from under us. Ordinarily, I didn't go into water over my head or where I couldn't see the bottom, but I was feeling very confident and exhilarated with the whole week, so I floated and dog paddled out into the middle of the lake.

Because the water came from the tall mountains, it was breathtakingly cold. I just had lunch and was one of the first campers to hurry back into the lake. I lay on my back floating gently out, just gazing at the clouds overhead and thinking what a wonderful world it was that day. My left calf muscle suddenly cramped and I instantly doubled up to rub the knots of muscle in the lower leg. When I did that, I quit floating and started to sink. Fear gripped me when I couldn't feel the bottom. I tried to get my body to float but the pain in my leg and the panic in my heart would not *cooperate. I swallowed water, I flung my arms like an egg beater, I looked around for someone close. There was no one near. As I felt the burning in my nose and throat from the water rushing in, I managed to audibly blurt out, "Oh God, help me!"*

Instantly, a man swam up from behind me and calmly said, "Put your hand on my shoulder." He didn't touch me, but just gave me that simple command. He was pale with blue eyes and light red hair. At the time, he didn't seem different, but was, oh so calm and reassuring.

I held onto his shoulder while he swam to the nearest pier, which was quite a long way. He said nothing else. When we reached the pier, a lifeguard waited with a large towel open for warmth. I climbed the wooden ladder to the pier and, shaking like a leaf in the wind, I wrapped up in the towel to get warm.

I turned to thank the kind man, but could see no one. I asked the lifeguard where he had gone and she looked puzzled as she told me there was no one but me.

For several minutes, I argued that a red-headed man had saved my life and helped me to the pier. She kept insisting that I came sputtering and splashing to the pier on my own. Finally, I could see that I wasn't going to change her mind and she certainly wasn't going to change mine, so I thanked her for her help and started toward my cabin.

I lay tearfully on my bunk that afternoon while the others played, swam, and joked. I went over the incident in my mind the rest of the afternoon. I realized that the man had looked different and he had spoken very calmly. Instead of reaching for me, he had told me what to do.

I went over and over the words, "God, help me!" I tried to think why the lifeguard couldn't see him and where he went after I was safely delivered.

I told no one else about the incident, but I pondered what had happened and asked God what it meant. From that time on, I've talked to God, not just in times of trouble, but about many things and He is faithful to answer. Never again have I seen an angel that I know of, but I have heard and read about them. I believe they are God's messengers sent to help us, rescue us, and bring us a message or warning.

Perhaps you can recall a time in your life where God supernaturally provided for your needs. He is called Jehovah-Jireh (Gen. 22:14) which means, "The Lord will provide." He often does this through His gracious ministering spirits, the angels.

Chapter 9

Angels Protect Us from Harm

Psalm 34:7 says, "The angel of the Lord encamps around those who fear him, and he delivers them." Elsewhere, God promises us protection by His angels: "For he will command his angels concerning you to guard you in all your ways; they will lift you up in their hands, so that you will not strike your foot against a stone" (Ps. 91:11–12). In Exodus 23:20, God said to Moses, "See, I am sending an angel ahead of you to guard you along the way and to bring you to the place I have prepared." So it is clear that a major role of angels is to guard and protect us.

Is there such a thing as a guardian angel? Many people speak of having a guardian angel. A friend of mine told me that his church teaches that you have a guardian angel that is with you from the time you are born until the time you die. That angel never leaves. My friend was even taught to pray regularly to his guardian angel.

What do the Scriptures say about a guardian angel who is with us from birth to death? Nothing. Nowhere in the Bible does it teach that there is one guardian angel assigned to every person. You won't even find the phrase "guardian angel" in the Bible. The closest thing to it is in Matthew 18:10. Jesus is speaking about little children. "See that you do not look down on one of these little ones. For I tell you that their angels in heaven always see the face of my Father in heaven." Jesus wasn't teaching about angels being with the children on earth, but being in heaven.

Let's keep our theology straight. Only God is present everywhere at once. Angels aren't. Satan, who is a fallen angel, is not. Only God is omnipresent. Angels in the Bible can't be in heaven and on earth at the same time. That is why Jacob saw angels ascending and descending on a ladder (Gen. 28:12). That's why Jesus told Nathanael in John 1:51 that he would "see heaven open, and the angels of God ascending and descending on the Son of Man."

The concept of one particular guardian angel who accompanies you all of your life is not taught in Scriptures. I don't believe in a singular guardian angel, but I do believe in the reality of many guardian angels. The Bible says God sends His angels to guard you, to keep you from hurting yourself at times.

I have received many stories of angel encounters and the majority of them deal with God's supernatural protection. Most of the accounts are of events that occurred when people were driving. People can recall events that happened thirty or forty years ago. They haven't been able to forget these encounters because they believe that God's angels were there to protect them. Following are some of those accounts.

Angel Encounter
by
Pam Morrison

I had an unusual experience a few years ago that I have always thought involved an angel's protection.

When Ray, my husband, was in medical school and residency, I taught school, and I was fortunate to live in the same neighborhood as my campus. One November day, though, I found myself in a rush-hour drive enroute to a conference in downtown Dallas. There was a pounding rain, very poor visibility, and the six-lane highway seemed jammed to capacity. I was driving alone in the left lane, approaching a rather winding section of the interstate when someone or something calmly compelled me to brake. I made no actual decision to do so; I just observed my foot moving to the brake, at which time I checked my rear-view mirror to find a gap between me and the car behind me, which signalled and moved to the next lane rather easily.

Since I was totally unaccustomed to driving in high-stress traffic situations, I had been feeling some anxiety, but when I started braking, I felt totally calm.

My car came to a complete stop just as I topped a "blind hill." Less than one car length in front of me was a parked car, with four people inside. There had been no possible way for me to have known it would be there; I had seen no brake lights before I braked.

I signalled right and I had to wait for an opportunity to change lanes and move on, and by the time I did, the stalled car in front of me had started and had driven on in safety.

Only after I was back in moving traffic did I realize how close I had come to potential disaster. My immediate reaction was a feeling that an angel had "taken charge" of my driving for a few crucial minutes. Otherwise, I cannot explain my behavior or my calm response throughout those few minutes.

I believe that God deals with us dramatically to help increase our faith and to improve our witness. My experience did both of those things for me.

Angel Encounter
by
Julie Burch

This is an angel story about my friend Julie Schultz. Julie was attending school at Vanderbilt and was living in a dorm on campus. At 11:30 on Thursday night, she real-

ized that she had forgotten to get some cash that she was going to need for the weekend. She left her dorm alone and drove to a nearby ATM machine.

West End Boulevard is a broad, busy thoroughfare that runs adjacent to the campus and leads into downtown. Julie drove down West End and pulled into a parking lot near a bank. There stood an ATM machine which was surrounded by bushes.

When she parked, she noticed a large man at the machine. After he finished his transaction, she got out of her car and began walking quickly to the machine. She felt very apprehensive in the dark lot and chided herself for waiting too late to get money. The man began walking toward Julie, instead of toward the street, and she was afraid that he was going to harm her. She lowered her eyes and continued walking and when he passed her, he said, "Just be careful. I'll be here if you need me." She was confused but relieved that he didn't bother her.

When she inserted her card, however, she realized that there was another man standing in the bushes, waiting to rob someone. She found herself panicking, but noticed that the large man had not left. He was still standing at the curb behind her. She took her money, ran to her car, jumped in, locked the doors and turned to look for the man, but he was nowhere in sight. Eager to thank him, she

*pulled out into West End, looked both ways,
but she did not see him. All of the traffic
lights were red and he had to have been
stopped at some point down the length of the
road, but he was not there. She is convinced
that the man was an angel.*

Angel Encounter
by
Rudy Turner

*There is no doubt in my mind that angels
exist. They are real. I have experienced their
presence.*

*My wife and I were on our way home from
visiting our daughter and her family who lived
in Rapid City, South Dakota. We were returning home through Wyoming, Colorado, and
New Mexico. The scenery was breathtaking.
My wife would occasionally ask me, "Where
are we now?" I had the map on the car seat
between us. When I picked up the map to
show her where we were, I took my eyes off
the road and the car ran off the pavement.
When I looked up, all I saw was a steel road
sign post in front of me. Some "force" turned
that steering wheel to get us back on the
pavement. The car stood up on two wheels
and then came back down on all four wheels
as I straightened out on the highway. Just as
I got control, a truck came over the hill. Had
it been three seconds sooner, we would have
been broadsided.*

*Had it not been for my guardian angel,
the force that took control of the car, I would
have run off the road into a canyon or been
broadsided by a truck.*

*Do I believe in angels? I sure do! Not only
do I have my "personal" guardian angel, but
I also have an angel of mercy who comforts
me in time of trouble and grief. Thank God for
angels.*

Angel Encounter
by
Vicki Garcia

When the children were very small, we
would take walks around the block. Charlie,
our dog, who is without a doubt the most
cowardly animal alive, was always taken with
us because he loved to go on walks. He was
absolutely useless and was never considered
as protection.

We were taking a street we had walked
many times. As we got within thirty feet of a
house where a big red Chow lived, I saw that
the gate to the backyard was ajar and off its
hinges. As I looked, the huge Chow appeared.
He was absolutely free and coming our way.
Chris, who was four at the time, was walking
a few feet ahead of me and I was carrying
two-year-old Ryan. The dog saw us only seconds after I saw him.

I prayed, "Lord, help us. I cannot protect the children." I spoke to Chris telling him the mean dog was loose and to walk quickly. When he looked and saw, he was frightened and started to run. Charlie was standing right beside this huge red Chow. I told Chris not to run, but it was too late. The Chow had the look of attack in his eyes. I knew I couldn't possibly place myself between them and if I could have, I had Ryan.

At that moment, Charlie began to growl and block this dog from attacking. Charlie jumped straight up in the air, blocking the oncoming dog. The Chow fell backward and got back up on his feet, shaking his head as if it had just run into a brick wall. By this time, I had grabbed Chris by the hand and we were safely across the street.

I thought of Elisha, who, when surrounded by a host of enemies told his servant, "Fear not, for they that be with us are more than they that be with them."

Angel Encounter
by
Name Withheld by Request

One of my first jobs out of college was in government. I was supposed to work eight to five daily, but meetings at night caused me to accumulate lots of extra hours. Periodically, I was given comp time instead of money.

A business friend asked me if I could work as a governess while she and her husband went on an out-of-town trip. They had a lovely home out in the country and several well-mannered children to watch. It sounded great.

The day the parents left, we had a big snowstorm. I was determined that the kids were going to go to school; the parents felt very strongly about that. While the kids and I were driving on this lonely country road, I realized we were in big trouble.

The road had a thin sheet of ice on it. There were no driveways or side streets to turn into, so I had to continue forward. The road curved over hills and had bridges over creeks. We went over one bridge, sliding a bit sideways. I was not even touching the gas pedal or brakes as the car came to a hill. I wondered how we would ever make it.

The car went halfway up the hill then started coming down sideways, sliding on the ice. I saw that we were headed for the edge of the road and a cliff beyond. There was a sheer drop with no trees to keep us from plummeting into the dense woods. I asked God to help me. I was responsible for the children, and I begged God not to let them suffer because of my lack of common sense.

The children were screaming and trying to open the doors of the car to jump out as we went off the road. The car was moving slowly but steadily towards the edge of the cliff. I felt very calm. An invisible presence was guiding the car. It stopped with the two front tires on the ground, and the back two tires hugging the edge, not on the ground. We got out of the car and marveled how close we came to falling off the edge. We thanked God for saving our lives.

Immediately, out of nowhere came a tow truck. The driver said that he forgot something and had to go home. He told us that it was a miracle he had come by; no one was on the roads but tow trucks and there was not a house for miles. We never would have made it had we tried walking to get help. The driver put chains on my tires and pulled the car off the cliff. He scratched his head, and said that I must have a guardian angel. I think so, too.

Angel Encounter
by
Cindy Knott

My story took place in 1989, in the Republic of Panama. A friend and I were on our way to go shopping in an area of Panama, and in order to get there, we had to walk through narrow streets. It was before the invasion of Panama and the Panamanian people were very anti-American. A certain area was marked off-limits to Americans, which we did not know about.

While we were walking to the shopping area, we took a street that we thought was a shortcut to the main road. We found out a few streets later that it was not a shortcut and we were lost in a very bad area.

None of the streets went straight and we had no idea which way to go and were becoming very frightened and very lost. We were walking down one street where some men were making comments to us as we walked by. We looked at each other and decided to stop there in the street and pray for God to help us because we didn't know which way to go.

Almost instantly, a short man dressed in nice clothing came up behind us. We were so amazed because we had not seen anyone there before. He spoke to us in English (which we thought was unusual, because hardly anyone in the area where we were going would speak English). He told us to follow him and stay as close to him as we could. We followed him down narrow, winding streets until we reached the corner of the street that we originally wanted to be on. (How did he know?)

He told us never to go back the way that we came because it was too dangerous. He told us the way to go back so that we would not get lost again. After that he turned around and walked away.

We turned to thank him, but he seemed to have disappeared because there was no one else around and he was gone. The man's image is as vivid to me today as it was in 1989.

Angel Encounter
by
Betty Turman

I had the most amazing experience with angels on 24 December 1990.

That Christmas season Tyler had a lot of ice. The main street was partially clear, but there was still some thin ice and slick patches. People had just turned on their headlights, and it was already dark at 5:00 P.M.

As I turned right onto the street, coming out of the grocery store's parking lot, I started into a skid. In a split second, I reminded myself to be very careful. I had looked ahead through my windshield and had seen the many lights of the oncoming traffic, and in my rear-view mirror, I saw more traffic bearing down on me. My car spun at least two full turns and finally stopped in the middle lane facing the opposite direction from which I had started.

There was no way on earth I could have survived without the intervention of angels. I felt as if in those three to five seconds, angels had halted the lights or the cars or done something to prevent a massive pileup. It seemed to me at that time that everything had stopped moving except me and my out-of-control car. There was no human way any of those cars could have stopped fast enough without skidding or going into a spin. I went home and told my husband that the arms of the Lord had been around me (I really did feel them) and the angels had protected me.

I've never had another experience quite like that one, but when you think about your "near misses" you know it's not luck, but God's love protecting you, sometimes with the help of angels.

Angel Encounter
by
Nancy Whittlock

One of my angel encounters was on a lovely April morning in 1985. I was driving to work, thinking what a beautiful day for the Lord to come again. As I turned off the Eighth Avenue north onto Twentieth Street, I had my window down, my parking card in my left hand, and my hand outside the window ready to put the card in the meter to go up and park as usual.

As I approached the crosswalk at the halfway section of Twentieth Street, I saw there was some sort of disturbance in the northbound lane. People were screaming and running. Two men were arguing. One man had a gun threatening the others. As I slowed my speed, it brought me within about twenty feet of the man with the gun. That man looked at *me and ran up to my car, pointed the gun directly in my face, pulled the trigger, once, twice, and three times. The gun clicked three times, but did not fire at all.*

Later it was decided the man must have thought I had something in my hand, maybe a gun, that would hurt him. He just saw my hand outside the window, but he probably didn't see what I had was only a card. The man cursed and shook the gun and motioned for me to get away from there.

Later, one of the detectives told me there were five bullets in the gun and three of them had been struck by the firing pin. They were good, live bullets, so they should have fired when struck. That detective told me I was the luckiest person he knew.

I said, "No, I am blessed."

Only God could have kept me from being killed that morning. It happened so suddenly, so unexpectedly, no human could have had any control over those bullets, only God. God had His angels around me to ward off those three bullets.

My second experience with the protection of angels was on Friday, 18 March 1988.

It was raining as I drove to work, going southbound on I-65. I rarely use my seat belts, but this morning something told me to buckle up, and I did.

I was in the extreme left lane approaching the I-65 interchange. As I reached the Six-

teenth Street entrance ramp (on the extreme
right of the highway), a black pick-up truck
came across three southbound lanes from that
entrance ramp and pulled directly in front of
me. He had not seen that the traffic ahead
was slowing down.

As he hit his brakes, I saw I was going to
hit his rear, so I swerved into the lane on my
right. He immediately pulled into the right
lane also. I applied my brakes to keep from
hitting him. My car went around one and a
half times. I skidded sideways and backwards
all at the same time and hit the concrete guard
rail broadside.

This all happened so fast, all I could do
was say, "Oh, dear God!" As I looked up,
ahead of me, which was actually the direction
from which I had just been coming, I thought
that in this heavy traffic lots of people are
going to be hurt. "Oh, dear God, help!" As I
sat there expecting to be hit by the oncoming
traffic, it seemed everything slowed down
around me. There was no traffic close to me.
When cars did get close to me, they were
traveling to my right very slowly and safely.
No other cars were involved.

Some construction men working on the
highway came to help me. They just knew I
was hurt and the left side of my car was
destroyed. They could not believe there was so
very little damage after I had hit that concrete wall broadside. Only my tires were dam-

aged and some chrome dented. Those men saw what had happened and said it was the strangest thing they had ever seen.

My insurance agent was very surprised when I explained what happened. He said I must have been hurt more than I realized. He had never believed in supernatural things, and he wasn't about to be convinced that angels had kept me from going off that hillside or kept me from being struck by the oncoming traffic.

I know what happened that morning. My driving ability had nothing to do with it. Again, God's angels were there to protect me from harm. I know angels travel with me and care for me daily. I just don't understand why God cares so much for me personally. I don't deserve this marvelous love and protection He affords me.

God has truly blessed and protected me and other members of my family through the years. Nobody can ever make me believe there are no angels. I know they are here for our protection and help.

Angel Encounter
by
Mary Deramus

I have had two significant incidents that I truly believe happened where angels had control.

The first was in 1953. It happened early one morning about 7:30, the time when traffic is usually the heaviest.

I had taken my husband, Euel, to work on East Erwin Street in Tyler and was returning to go across town to my job on the west side of town. It was misting rain, and the streets were wet and slick. I was stopped by the red lights at the Houston and Beckham intersection and was forced to stop on a slight incline.

As I was sitting still, headed west, all of a sudden my car began to slide. My car slid slowly to the right, turned completely around, and stopped when the rear end of the car was facing west.

The car kept moving backwards, and as I was going into the slide, a voice as clear as day said, "Take your foot off the brake," which I did. My hands were on the wheel, but I was not guiding the car. I could feel the wheel turning, but my hands were not guiding it. I never looked, nor saw where the car was heading. I only knew it was sliding backwards. It was as if I were in slow motion.

All at once, this same voice said, "Put your foot on the brake and stop the car, now!" I immediately put my foot on the brake and stopped the car. When I looked around, I was only inches away from hitting one of the two houses that were located at that time, beside the railroad tracks. There was no curb, and both houses were right by the street with hardly any front yard. A lady was standing on the front porch of the house where I stopped. She told me she just knew I was going to run right into her yard.

A man who had witnessed my car's maneuvers as he approached the red light pulled up beside me to see if I was okay. He told me he had never seen better driving in his whole life. I said, "Thank you, but it was not me driving!"

At the busiest time of the morning, while my car was sliding, there was not one other car passing at the intersection. Had there been, this could have been a very tragic traffic accident. I thank God for His "guiding" angel that day.

Angel Encounter
by
Marilyn Jones

My son, Jody, who was almost eleven, was at the swimming pool. I had often left him there with one of my two teenagers who were seventeen and nineteen at the time.

About thirty minutes after I had left him, my seventeen year old came home and said Jody was not ready to come home. I needed to get groceries so I asked my husband to go and stay with Jody for a little while. He told me that he could not stay because he had too much to do, but that he would get Jody and bring him home.

Even though I knew Jody was a very good swimmer, I still had a mother's concern. I had heard teachings about our ministering spirits, and I called on them to minister and encamp around him for a couple of hours. A real peace came over me.

When Jody came home that afternoon, he seemed unusually quiet. I asked him why he was so quiet. He said, "Well, while I was at the pool playing with my friends there was a man standing on the deck. He looked like he was motioning to me and I got out of the pool and went up to him to see what had happened. I didn't go all the way.

"He said, 'I have come to protect you.'

"I said, 'All right.' I went back to the pool and asked my friend if he saw the man I was talking to but he said he didn't see anybody."

Jody said, "Mama, I think he was an angel." I asked Jody to describe the man and he said he looked as if he was about twenty-five or twenty-six, had blond hair, and was dressed in a white outfit that looked like a two-piece suit, but when he got close he could tell it was one piece. He also said he had blue eyes and did not wear shoes.

Jody did not know I had prayed for ministering spirits to protect him, but after he shared with me his encounter that afternoon, I told him what I had prayed.

Angel Encounter
by
Diana Mcallister

On Friday, 13 January 1984, my son Joseph was involved in a horrible and almost fatal accident. Joseph was two and one-half years old at the time. We were shopping in a major shopping mall in San Antonio. A belt rack fell, striking my son in the head.

The rack fell in such a way that it sent two, four-inch prongs into his brain and crushed his skull. One of the prongs went through his right eye, the other through the right temple area just over the ear. He also suffered massive bleeding in two areas deep within the brain.

When EMS arrived, I had already performed CPR and had him breathing on his own. They bandaged both his eyes as well as the fractured skull. Joseph was comatose and responsive only to deep pain. He was then rushed to the children's hospital where he spent the next three months in intensive care.

Joseph was never expected to survive. The nurses wondered each night as they went home if he would be there the next day. Two weeks after his first surgery, it was discovered that his brain had herniated into the right eye socket and had been exposed to bacteria and germs for the past two weeks. He underwent a second brain surgery.

The doctor told me that if he survived, he would be a vegetable and most definitely severely mentally retarded.

Throughout the time that Joseph was hospitalized, people would walk by his bed, stop, and ask if they could touch him, pray near him, etc., because they could see the aura of Jesus around him.

The night of the accident, I called a friend and asked her to pray for Joseph. I, too, said the following prayer, "Lord, if my son cannot lead a normal, fulfilling life, please take him with You." I knew immediately that Jesus would spare his life and he would be fine.

However, because the doctors felt I was hysterical and in denial, they tried to sedate me with valium. It never took effect. Joseph was in everyone's prayers throughout the country that fateful night. I received letters from strangers telling me that they were keeping him in their prayers. I even received letters from a third grade class in Kentucky saying they had heard of Joseph and were praying for him.

Six months after the accident, Joseph was back in the hospital due to complications. He was placed in a room over the emergency room. As we were waiting for the doctor to come, Joseph heard an ambulance enter the E.R. He wanted to see it so I carried him to the window.

He exclaimed, *"That's the ambulance I rode in when I died!"*

I said, *"You never died."*

He said, *"Yes I did. I died in a store and you rode with me in that and you were crying. And then this doctor made me come back. I screamed and screamed and Jesus came and took me to this place so it wouldn't hurt any more."*

The doctor, who had just come into the room while Joseph was talking, started asking him many questions. For a while, Joseph described things that he could not have known or seen because his eyes were bandaged or because he was under anesthesia. When the doctor tried to pin him down and dispute that it was Jesus, Joseph simply stopped talking about it.

The doctor said that by the time Joseph is old enough to understand it and to tell the truth, he won't remember it. The doctor is of the Jewish faith and could not believe that Jesus exists.

I believe Joseph spoke the truth as a three year old knew and understood it. I had spoken of Jesus to Joseph since before he was born. I believe that Joseph was with the angels during the worst time of this ordeal. He came out of it with such a peace, calmness, and such a beautiful smile that he could have been nowhere else.

Joseph should not be here today, but he is. He has overcome every obstacle imaginable. He is not blind and he is not mentally retarded. He can walk, even though he was paralyzed in the beginning. He has many health problems and is not expected to live beyond his teens, but then Jesus has not said when he would go. Professionals in the medical field cannot explain Joseph's presence. God is truly in charge.

Angel Encounter
by
Sylvia Best

In the spring of 1988, I had a spiritual experience that I could not explain, although I knew that it was very real.

My husband had cancer and had become very ill as the cancer spread all over his body. He was bedridden and was almost helpless. I had help during the day, but nights I was alone with him. I had a hospital bed for him and a regular bed in the same room for me. I worried that I could not even get him out of the bed if the house caught fire.

Late one night while I was sitting on the side of the bed, worrying about what I could do, I saw a soft silver cloud settle and hover over my husband's body, staying there only a very short time. Then it went away just as it came. It was different than any light that I had ever seen.

We lived in the woods at the dead end of a road with no cars passing, no light outside. I knew that it was from God because of the peace that I felt. Throughout God's Word you find many, many examples of how angels shielded God's people from harm. The Bible tells us in Daniel 6 that an angel was the one who kept the mouths of the lions shut when Daniel was in the lions' den.

Chapter 10

Angels Preside at Our Death

Have you ever thought of angels as "heavenly undertakers"? Actually, you could call them "uppertakers." According to what the Lord Jesus said in Luke, angels are present at the time we die. They are the ones who carry our soul and spirit into heaven. Luke 16:22 states, "The time came when the beggar died and the angels carried him to Abraham's side." A blessed truth is that angels are present when we depart this life. They are the ones who escort our souls, our spirits into heaven itself.

Some misinformed individuals believe that there is nothing supernatural about angels. They think angels are kind human beings who act angelic. There have been books written in which authors describe angels as only individuals who do nice things for others.

Although, it may be possible for mortals to act angelic at times, the Bible teaches that angels are supernatural beings whom God has given us for specific tasks. A human being might deliver a message from God through the Word and that would be an angelic ministry. A fellow human being might protect somebody from harm and might even help an individual understand God's Word. But, a person cannot carry someone's soul and spirit into heaven. Only a supernatural being from God can do that.

Joan Watkins and Jeff Bowman each share about angels presiding at their mothers' deaths in the following encounters.

Angel Encounter
by
Joan Watkins

I am a Christian and have always taken by faith the ministering of angels. I have always been thrilled by these seemingly magical events. My mother, Mrs. Lora Ann Uptain, passed away after a year's fight with cancer. She was forty years old, the mother of five, and a Baptist minister's wife. Mother had many friends who stayed faithfully by our side and provided prayers, visits, and gifts. Many of these gifts came in the form of plants or flowers. It was late November, just days before her death, when an aunt and uncle wired a pink poinsettia to the hospital room. Each leaf was polished with silver glitter and it was a beautiful plant.

For months our family had prayed for life and healing for Mother, but by this time we prayed for the Lord to take her home. She had given the Lord her life on earth and had served

Him. We could no longer selfishly pray for the Lord to leave her with us. Three or four weeks before her death, she began having great difficulty breathing.

The morning before Mother died, I was sitting by her bedside holding her hand. We sat quietly, not saying much for several hours. I stared at her, she stared across the room at the pink poinsettia. In an effort to help her relax, I moved the plant to the foot of her bed.

She again set her gaze on the poinsettia as I took my seat and held her hand. To get her attention I would have to call her name several times. As I sat there, I prayed for her suffering to be over and for the Lord to give her comfort in her last hours.

She began to say, "The beautiful faces! Oh! The beautiful faces." A smile came over her face that stayed with her every minute she was awake until she died. In her sleep, she would moan from the pain but when awake, she maintained that she felt fine. She tried very hard to be brave in spite of the pain.

Mother died that evening with my father, older sister, and brother-in-law by her side. She took a deep breath and smiled as if relieved to get a full breath of air into her lungs, and the Lord took her home.

I still long to be held when I need my mother, and I remember holding her during her sickness. But, I'm always reminded that

I have the everlasting arms of God to hold me, and they are holding my mother. I can't be any closer to her than that.

In answering our prayers, God used the ministering of angels. I believe the "beautiful faces" that brought mother so much comfort and a smile to her face were the faces of angels. I am sure that these weren't the only ministering spirits bestowed upon us, but the recollection is the most vivid in my mind and dearest to my heart.

Angel Encounter
by
Jeff Bowman

In World War II, while I was overseas fighting, I always felt the closeness of my mother. As I was leaving home, she reminded me to "remember to pray." She prayed and looked to God daily to keep me safe and bring me home.

Mother's health was not good at that time; she suffered from a heart condition. She found great strength in prayer, encouraging me to "remember to pray." Every day I was gone from her, I prayed to God, "Please keep her on earth long enough for me to return home." It was also those prayers that brought me safely through the war. Prayers were answered over and over again.

The day finally came that I returned to the states and saw my mother and father again.

It was a wonderful reunion to be at home with the both of them once again.

Even after I married and moved to Crockett, Texas, Mother continued to have attacks with her heart from time to time. Each time I would pray, "God, I don't want to give Mother up just yet. Please leave her with us just a little longer."

God answered those prayers so many times. She would get better and be able to be up and about for a while, then another attack would weaken her once again. I always thanked God for leaving her with us "just a little longer."

Then the day came that I received a telephone call from my brother-in-law in Trinity, that Mother was "nearly gone." If I wanted to see her alive, I should come and come quickly, for she was barely alive.

I immediately got into the car to drive the twenty-eight miles to Trinity, in hopes that I would arrive in time to spend just a few minutes with her before she died. As I drove, I prayed to God, asking Him to leave her with us just a little longer.

"I'm not ready to give her up Lord."

As I drove on, I was reminded that she was very ill and I was being selfish to ask for her to live. Then I prayed once more saying, "God, I know I'm being selfish by asking for her to live when I know that she will never really be well." I then said, "God, I want only that Your will be done." After I prayed that prayer, God spoke to me and said, "Jeff, your mother is gone. She won't be there when you get to her."

There was a deep sadness that came over me for just a moment, then a sweet peace. I knew God had taken her soul to rest with Him.

When I drove up in the front yard, I was met on the porch by my father who said, "Son, you're too late; she is gone."

I said, "Yes, I know."

I walked into the house where my sisters met me. They told me Mother was in her bedroom, for the funeral director had not picked up her body yet. I walked on down the hall, into her bedroom, and stopped at the foot of her bed. There, standing by the side of her bed, was an angel. I didn't look at mother, but continued looking at the angel who paused for a few seconds and suddenly disappeared up, up through the ceiling until she was out of sight. She didn't speak, nor did I, but she came as a sign to me (no one else could see her) that she had taken Mother's soul with her to reign with God in heaven.

After thirty years, I still miss my mother. I have that blessed assurance of knowing where my mother is. My father joined her a few years later. I know that they are waiting for me, and I will join them when God calls me home for the greatest reunion of all.

*   *   *   *   *

As you read about how angels protect us from harm, you may have reflected upon your own experiences and thought, "I had a loved one who was a Christian. He had an accident and God didn't protect him. Why wasn't he protected? Where were the angels when my loved one or my friend suffered and died?" I do not understand it; all I know is that sometimes angels are there to protect and sometimes they aren't. According to God's sovereign will, He sometimes allows good people to suffer and die.

If you really struggle, write down this Scripture reference, Hebrews 11:35. Chapter 11 of Hebrews tells about all the great saints of God, the roll call of faith, and the supernatural delivery of many. The last part of the passage tells about all of those that were not supernaturally delivered, those who suffered from the sword and were cut in half, stoned, and died. Then it says, "so that they might gain a better resurrection."

If I understand the Christian life, it is wonderful to be protected supernaturally and to be delivered, but for Christians, sometimes it is even better to go on and be with Jesus. Paul said, "For to me, to live is Christ and to die is gain" (Phil. 1:21). So, on some occasions, the angels are there, but God's will is not for them to protect. God's will for them is to carry that person's soul and spirit into heaven. Angels do preside at our deaths.

As I was writing this chapter in 1992, I received a call that one of our deacons, Wayne Goff, put on his pajamas, went to bed, fell asleep, and woke up with Jesus. As his wife and I spoke that morning, we talked about how, sometime during the night, the angels had come and visited Wayne and carried his soul and spirit into heaven.

Chapter 11

Angels Praise God with Us

Angels are experts at praising God. Psalm 148:2 contains this call to praise: "Praise him, all his angels, praise him, all his heavenly hosts." The phrase in the Bible, "heavenly hosts," is a term to describe the angelic armies. Angels participate with all of creation to praise God.

We are told in the Book of Revelation that there are some angels that are created only to praise God; they stay at the throne of God and praise him night and day. But, there are other angels who shuttle back and forth to heaven. Sometimes they are in the presence of the Father and sometimes they are here on earth. I believe that those angels praise God when they are in His presence as well as when they are here.

When we gather to worship and praise the Lord, the angels are present with us. There is something about an atmosphere of praise and worship that is conducive to the activity and the presence of angels. I believe that if God could open our spiritual eyes, most of us would be scared to death. If, however, he could open our spiritual eyes as we are worshipping and praising the Lord, I believe we could see God's angels encamped all around this place, praising God with us.

In the Book of Revelation, chapters 4 and 5, we read that one day when we are in heaven we will gather around the throne of the Lamb and praise Him saying, "Worthy is the Lamb, who was slain." Angels have known the character of Jesus since they were created. They will join with us in this mighty doxology of tribute to Jesus.

Angels have the ability to rejoice. Do you know what makes the angels rejoice? According to the Lord Jesus, when one sinner repents, the angels rejoice. He said in Luke 15:10, "In the same way, I tell you, there is rejoicing in the presence of the angels of God over one sinner who repents."

After reading about the ministry of these supernatural beings, you may be a little skeptical. You may be wondering if you can believe everything that you have read. The Bible is neither logical nor illogical—it is supralogical. It exceeds human understanding. You can't always figure out God's activity in a test tube. You can't work it out on a computer. Perhaps you need to drop your intellectual questioning and say, "By faith I believe in God and I believe in what God's Word says about Him." Jesus said that you must become as a little child to become a Christian.

You may have become so intellectually skeptical that when you read these stories about angels you say, "I'm not too sure about that." You have to become as a little child and in childlike faith say, "God, I don't understand You, and I don't understand all Your ways, but I trust You. I believe You. Not only with my life, but with my eternity."

There will always remain a mystery about God's ways that we cannot unravel. He says, "As the heavens are higher than the earth, so are my ways higher than your ways and my thoughts than your thoughts" (Isa. 55:9).

God sends His mighty angels to minister to saints in a variety of ways. This poem describes how God loves us so much that He blesses our lives through His angels.

How I Love You

My dear child, how I love you,
And I want you to know
That I'll bless your life richly.
Through these troubles, you'll grow.

I've seen how you've struggled
To live with life's pains,
But, in your trusting of Me,
There are blessings to gain.

You'll walk through some rivers,
But they won't overcome you.
My angels are all around
To carry you right through.

My angels surround you.
They are friends in your life.
I put them there daily
To ease with your strife.

Every struggle you face
Doesn't happen in vain.
The angels are watching
To assist with your pain.

Keep praising and smiling
And joyfully living.
Allow the angels to touch you
With my tender giving.

The friendships and love
You are feeling each day,
I put there to teach you,
And to show you My way.

You are sweeter to Me
Than precious silver or gold.
The angels will be there.
Through them, My hand you will hold.

My dear child, how I love you,
And I want you to know.
That I'll bless your life richly.
Through these troubles, you'll grow.

                                    —Harriet Renner

Section IV
The Might of Angels

Angels are not wimps who only decorate the front of Christmas cards. In God's Word, they are described as warriors who comprise the "host of heaven."

Chapter 12

The Army of Angels

Most people envision angels to be sweet, gentle beings; however, the Bible describes angels as mighty warriors of God. We read in Psalm 103:20, "Praise the Lord you his angels, you mighty ones who do his bidding, who obey his word." Angels excel in strength to obey God's commandments. They are always listening for the command of their Commander in Chief.

In 2 Peter 2:11, we find another Scripture that teaches us about the supreme, exceeding might of angels, God's ministering spirits, "Yet even angels, although they are stronger and more powerful, do not bring slanderous accusations against such beings in the presence of the Lord." Angels are stronger and more powerful than the armies of man. Even though angels are mighty in strength, they often choose to display meekness.

Also, in Jude, verse 9, we see another reference to the mighty strength of angels. "But even the archangel Michael, when he was disputing with the devil about the body of Moses, did not dare to bring a slanderous accusation against him, but said, 'The Lord rebuke you!' "

The word *dispute* means to fight. Moses died at the age of 120 years. Deuteronomy 34:6 says that God buried him. In His perfect plan, God wanted to bring Moses' body to heaven so that Moses would be able to stand on the Mount of Transfiguration with Jesus. Apparently the devil, who is the ruler over the grave, did not agree to this plan, so Michael and the devil fought over it.

It is comforting to see that the devil was no match for Michael, the archangel, because Moses did appear with Jesus on the Mount of Transfiguration. So, in the Bible, angels are described as exceptionally powerful warriors.

Our God is not a God of confusion, but rather a God of supreme order. God has organized angels into an army of many divisions and ranks. If you have ever served in the military, you understand the importance of organization and rank. You know the difference between a private, sergeant, lieutenant, captain, major, and soldiers, up to general and commander in chief. In God's army, there is also order and division.

When Joshua was preparing to attack Jericho, the Bible says that he met a man in a shining garment, obviously an angel. Joshua did not recognize the man as an angel so he asked him, "Are you for us or for our enemies?"

"Neither," he replied, "but as commander of the army of the Lord I have now come"

(Josh. 5:14). The word *host* is used to describe a powerful army. This angel was a captain in God's angelic army.

As I have mentioned before, one danger about the study of angels is that some people become so obsessed with the presence of angels that they come dangerously close to worshipping them. Angels do not care to be recognized, and they become alarmed if they are worshipped. In Revelation, when the Apostle John falls down to worship, the angel quickly corrects his mistake. The angel says to John, "See that you do not do that, for I am your fellow servant and of your brethren the prophets and of those that keep the sayings of this book: worship God" (Rev. 19:10).

Terms Reserved for God

There are three words that we use in reference to God that never should be used to describe angels.

First, God is *omnipresent*. That means that the presence of God permeates every part of the universe. Angels are not omnipresent; they cannot be everywhere at once. Even the devil, who is a fallen angel, cannot be everywhere. People often assume that Satan can be everywhere at once; that is a dangerous belief because it ascribes to a fallen angel an attribute that belongs only to the living God. The Bible tells us that "the devil prowls around like a roaring lion looking for someone to devour" (1 Pet. 5:8).

Second, God is *omniscient*. That means God knows everything. We are mistaken if we think that angels know everything. Again, even Satan, the fallen angel, does not know everything. He is smarter than most of us, certainly he is clever and subtle, but don't ever say that he is omniscient. Satan only knows what God allows him to know.

Third, God is *omnipotent*. That means God is all-powerful. Angels are powerful, but only God is all-powerful. Likewise, Satan is not all-powerful.

Almost five hundred years ago, Martin Luther penned that wonderful hymn, "A Mighty Fortress Is Our God." Luther reminded us that there is a great spiritual warfare occurring around us. When we sing this song, we often miss the point of the message. In the first two verses, Martin Luther wrote about God's greatness, then he began to talk about the devil.

> For still our ancient foe
> Doth seek to work us woe;
> His craft and power are great,
> And armed with cruel hate,
> On earth is not his equal.

Martin Luther is correct: Satan is powerful, and no person on earth can match his diabolical power. However, God is much more powerful. The beautiful hymn climaxes with that recognition.

That word above all earthly pow'rs,
No thanks to them, abideth;
The Spirit and the gifts are ours
Thro' him who with us sideth:
Let goods and kindred go,
This mortal life also;
The body they may kill:
God's truth abideth still,
His kingdom is forever.

So, while angels are intelligent and mighty, they are not worthy of our worship. Neither do they desire our worship.

Chapter 13

An Army of Divisions

The Bible speaks of an archangel. Michael as the archangel can be considered as a type of prime minister, commander, and chief (Jude 9). We often think that there are several archangels, but the Bible identifies only Michael as the archangel.

In his seventeen-volume epic entitled *Paradise Lost*, John Milton incorrectly identifies Gabriel as one of the archangels. The Bible never gives this title to Gabriel.

Interestingly, only three angels are named in the NIV Bible—Michael, Gabriel, and Lucifer, the fallen angel. All of the angels have names, but we are not given the names of any except these three.

Michael is not often seen in the Scriptures. In Jude 9, he is mentioned as having contended with Satan over the body of Moses. This was discussed in chapter twelve.

The Bible also teaches that when Jesus returns, Michael will shout (1 Thess. 4:16). This verse says that there will be the sound of the trumpet as well. Popular music has erroneously identified Gabriel as the angel who will blow the horn. While this belief may be popular in the French Quarter of New Orleans, it is foreign to the Bible. We have no idea who will play the trumpet.

Seraphim

The Bible speaks of another division of angels besides the archangel. These are the seraphim. In Hebrew, when the suffix "im" is added, it makes that word plural. One of these angels would be called a seraph, and more than one would be called seraphim. In Isaiah 6, we are introduced to these angelic creatures. Isaiah sees a vision of the greatness of God and part of his vision includes the seraphim. He describes them in the following way:

> Above him were seraphs, each with six wings: with two wings they covered their faces, with two they covered their feet, and with two they were flying. And they were calling to one another: "Holy, holy, holy is the Lord Almighty; the whole earth is full of his glory." (Isa. 6:2–3)

Certainly, this is where many people get the idea that angels have wings. However, we will see later that seldom are ordinary angels described as possessing wings. What was the job of the seraphim? They were created to praise and worship God. In Revelation 4:6–8, the Apostle John sees four heavenly creatures praising God. These four living creatures are also described as having six wings. Their job is to surround the throne of God and to render continual praise to Him. John wrote, "Day and night they never stop saying: Holy, Holy, Lord God Almighty, who was, and is, and is to come" (Rev. 4:8). Many scholars consider these to be the same heavenly beings in Isaiah 6.

Cherubim

Beside the archangel and seraphim, the Bible also speaks of cherubim. As with seraphim, cherub would be singular with cherubim being plural. Cherubim are mentioned many more times in Scripture than seraphim. In Genesis 3, after Adam and Eve had been cast out of the Garden of Eden, God placed cherubim there to guard the tree of life with the flaming sword (Gen. 3:24).

When God gave Moses the details for the construction of the tabernacle, He left instructions to place replicas of cherubim on top of the ark of the covenant. This mercy seat that sat on the top of the ark was designed so that two cherubim were facing with their wings outstretched. According to Ezekiel, cherubim have four wings as opposed to seraphim who possess six (Ezek. 10:21). In the curtain of the tabernacle, there were figures of cherubim.

Ezekiel refers to cherubim nineteen times in his prophecy. The tenth chapter of Ezekiel is an amazing description of these cherubim. This is the source of the old Negro spiritual "A Wheel Within A Wheel." Ezekiel describes a fantastic vision of a wheel within a wheel with the inner wheel turning one way and the outer wheel turning another way. This entire vision is filled with lights and begins to fly, with the ability to move suddenly in every direction.

In his book *Angels, God's Secret Agents*, Billy Graham refers to the fact that many people believe that what some individuals have seen and considered to be UFOs through the years may literally be a vision of these cherubim. If you take, for instance, the description of a very credible airline crew who saw some strange lights in the sky, their description of the color and size of what they saw is amazingly similar to the description in Ezekiel 10.

You may be thinking, "Are you saying that all UFOs are angels?" No, not at all. I am just pointing out that many people, including some of the most respectable biblical scholars, have recognized the similarities with Ezekiel 10. So, some of these UFOs actually could be AFOs—Angelic Flying Objects.

Ordinary Angels

While we do not know a great deal about Michael, the archangel, seraphim, and cherubim, the Bible is full of references to ordinary angels. Some people refer to this group as the holy angels, or common angels. For sure, there is nothing common about them. Gabriel would be considered one of these ordinary angels. He is always seen in the Scriptures as a messenger angel. His name means "God's hero." He is seen four times in Scripture. On two occasions, Gabriel appears to Daniel and ministers to him in his time of need. In the New Testament, Gabriel appears to Zacharias, the soon-to-be father of John the Baptist.

There is no indication that Zacharias was overwhelmed by the vision of Gabriel. In fact, he even disagrees with Gabriel's prediction. When Gabriel predicts that he will become a father, Zacharias scoffs at the idea by saying that he and his wife are too old. As a result, Gabriel had the power to take away the voice of Zacharias for the next nine months.

The most important appearance of Gabriel occurs when he appears to a virgin named Mary and predicts that she will give birth to God's Son, the Messiah. There are many other references to the appearance and activity of God's ordinary holy angels. The number of this group is never determined. In Revelation, John saw ten thousand times ten thousand angels. That is a hundred million angels. But, this is not a final definitive number. It is also a term that is often used to describe "beyond number." (See Rev. 5:11.)

Chapter 14

An Army of Destruction

When you recognize that angels comprise a great army for God, you begin to see many references in the Bible to their destructive strength. Angels often bring God's judgment upon a sinful nation. Here are five examples of the destructive power of God's angelic army.

Angels Visited Sodom

In Genesis 19, two angels came to the city of Sodom. This was a highly immoral city because of the widespread practice of homosexuality. The angels came to visit Lot, the cousin of Abraham. The city had become so vile in its homosexuality that the men of the city wanted to engage in sexual relations with the angels. The angels' message to Lot reveals their amazing strength. "We are going to destroy this place. The outcry to the Lord against its people is so great that he has sent us to destroy it" (Gen. 19:13).

God had given Abraham a chance for the city to be spared, but when Abraham was unable to find even ten righteous men in Sodom, God's judgment was inevitable. It is good to know that ours is a loving God, full of mercy and kindness, and He always gives people space to repent. However, Sodom refused to repent, so angels were the agents of God's destruction. There was a fiery end to a city that had burned already with immoral, unnatural lust.

The Angel of Death at the Passover

In Exodus 12, we read of another example of the destructive power of God's angels. When Pharaoh refused to allow the children of Israel to leave, God sent a series of plagues upon the land. Pharaoh's heart was hardened, and he continued stubbornly to resist the plea of Moses. A final deadly plague was unleashed by God. Specific instructions were given for every Hebrew family to kill a lamb, sprinkle the blood on the door post and lintel, enter into the house, and eat the meat from the lamb. Any family not following these instructions would suffer the death of their first born—men and animals (Exod. 12:12). God warned that every house that was covered with the blood would be spared the judgment of death. Once again, we see that our loving Lord offers a way to escape judgment.

That night, God's mighty passover angel visited the nation as God promised. In 1 Corinthians 10:10, this angel is called "the destroying angel." This angel of death "passed over" the home protected by the blood of the lamb. That night in Egypt, many thousands of people were killed because they refused to obey God's clear warning to release the Israelites from bondage.

David's Prayer that Prevented Destruction

In 2 Samuel 24, we read about an unusual occurrence demonstrating the might of angels. God became angry at the nation of Israel because of their continual rebellion and idolatry. As a result, He sent one angel to deliver His judgment. Seventy thousand people were destroyed by that mighty angel (2 Sam. 24:15–16). In addition, the angel was poised over the city of Jerusalem ready to destroy the entire population. Fortunately, when King David saw the angel, he prayed earnestly to God that his judgment might be held back. David confessed that he was personally guilty for the sins of the nation. In a spirit of humility and meekness, he asked God to punish him, but to spare the nation. This is one of the most touching examples in the Bible of intercessory prayer. As a result of the confession and repentance of David, God decided not to destroy the entire population of Jerusalem.

The Syrian Massacre

There is an exciting story in 2 Kings 19 of the army of Israel being utterly surrounded and outnumbered by the Assyrians. The

Assyrian army was comprised of 180,000 soldiers, who were laying siege to the army of Israel. However, during the night a single warrior-angel went out to face the Assyrian army.

> That night the angel of the Lord went out and put to death a hundred and eighty-five thousand men in the Assyrian camp. When the people got up the next morning—there were all the dead bodies! So Sennacherib king of Assyria broke camp and withdrew. He returned to Nineveh and stayed there. (2 Kings 19:35–36)

Are you beginning to see the absolute power and might of God's angels?

The Death of Herod Agrippa

You may be saying, "Well, all of that is Old Testament teaching. We are New Testament Christians. Is there any example after the birth of Jesus?" The answer to that can be found in Acts 12. Herod Agrippa was an egotistical maniac. He considered himself to be a king, although he was only a middle-management governmental official. He was sitting on a throne receiving the worship and adoration of the population. In Acts 12:23 we read, "Immediately, because Herod did not give praise to God, an angel of the Lord struck him down, and he was eaten by worms and died." That should serve as a stern warning to all of us to guard against arrogance.

These are five examples of the destructive power of angels, and there are many others in the Bible. Does this sound like angels are nice, sweet, little creatures? When we someday meet the angels in heaven, I believe we will recognize them as formidable warriors.

The Future Judgment

Jesus makes it clear that the angels will be the agents of judgment in a future harvest. As I mentioned earlier, this is most apparent in the parable of the wheat and the weeds. In this story, a farmer planted wheat and was expecting a good crop. However, in the middle of the night an enemy entered the field and planted weeds among the good wheat. As they began to grow, the strategy of the enemy became apparent. Although the servants wanted to go out and pull up the weeds, the master cautioned them to wait. Instead, he insisted that the wheat and the weeds grow together and at harvest time they would be separated and the weeds would be burned. In Matthew 13:37–42, Jesus explains the role of angels in judgment.

> He answered, "The one who sowed the good seed is the Son of Man. The field is the world, and the good seed stands for the sons of the kingdom. The weeds are the sons of the evil one, and the enemy who sows them is the devil. The harvest is the end of the age, and the harvesters are angels. As the weeds are

pulled up and burned in the fire, so it
will be at the end of the age. The Son of
Man will send out his angels, and they
will weed out of his kingdom everything
that causes sin and all who do evil. They
will throw them into the fiery furnace,
where there will be weeping and gnashing of teeth."

The angels will be the ones sent forth to
gather the wicked to be punished for eternity
in a place called hell. Remember, it was never
God's original plan to send anyone to hell. We
are told that hell was prepared for the devil
and his angels (Matt. 25:41). Angels, indeed
comprise an army of destruction.

Chapter 15

An Army of Deliverance

It is somewhat scary to think about the destructive power of angels, but the good news is that, for God's children, they are also an army of deliverance. Angels are involved in spiritual warfare and they are fighting on our behalf. They encourage us and enable us to be victorious in spiritual warfare.

For example, at the same moment that the angels were coming to destroy Sodom, they were also coming to deliver Lot and his family. They announced that judgment was coming, and they offered to lead them out of danger. In Genesis 19:15–16 we read,

> With the coming of dawn, the angels urged Lot, saying, "Hurry! Take your wife and your two daughters who are here, or you will be swept away when the city is punished." When he hesitated, the men grasped his hand and the hands of his wife and of his two daughters and led them safely out of the city, for the Lord was merciful to them.

That is a good example of the ministry of deliverance that angels perform. Many times angels rescue us from danger.

As I mentioned in an earlier chapter, spiritual warfare is invisible. If you could open your eyes to see the spiritual realities all around us, you would be shocked to see the intensity and the scope of warfare between angels and demons. In Daniel 10, we gain a glimpse of this invisible warfare. Daniel reported that he had been praying for twenty-one days. An angel came to him and shared the reason why his prayers were seemingly unanswered for a period. The angel said, "Your words were heard, and I am come in response to them. But the prince of the Persian kingdom resisted me twenty-one days. Then Michael, one of the chief princes, came to help me, because I was detained there with the King of Persia" (Dan. 10:13). Many have taken this to mean that the devil was resisting the prayers of Daniel and that Michael and the angel speaking to Daniel fought against the "prince" (a demon) for the prayer to be answered.

When we are on our knees praying, we are involved in great spiritual warfare. Angels respond to the prayers of God's people for deliverance. That is why the Bible says, "For our struggle is not against flesh and blood, but against rulers, against authorities, against the powers of this dark world and against the spiritual forces of evil in the heavenly realms" (Eph. 6:12).

Sometimes invisible spiritual warfare even affects earthly warfare. There are many accounts coming from World War II of such a connection. I believe that Adolf Hitler was a man deeply influenced by Satan and his demons. His plot to kill the Jews and conquer the world was hatched in hell. He was not a highly intelligent man, but there seemed to be an invisible force promoting him to his place of prominence. Many people believe that the prayers of God's faithful people during World War II were instrumental in bringing about victory for the allies.

In his book, *Angels: God's Secret Agents*, Billy Graham recounts many unusual events from World War II. In the beginning of the war, one of the main reasons that England was not invaded was because of the Royal Air Force. The RAF was constantly flying missions against Germany and attacking the bombers that were flying toward England. This understaffed group of pilots often flew beyond their physical limits of endurance with equipment that mechanically was unfit to fly.

After the war, Chief Air Marshall Lloyd Hugh Dowding attended a victory celebration. In the presence of royalty, the prime minister, and many dignitaries, he told of fliers who, having been hit by enemy fire were either incapacitated or dead. Yet, their planes kept on flying and fighting. On occasion, British pilots would see a figure still operating the controls. Mr. Dowding said he believed angels had actually flown some of the planes whose pilots sat dead in their cockpits.[4]

Air Chief Lloyd H. Dowding believes that angels were flying those airplanes and were instrumental in the air victory over Germany. Prayer has a great impact on the outcome of spiritual warfare. Jerry Gardner experienced this truth in the following encounter.

Angel Encounter
by
Jerry Gardner

On 3 October 1984, I was a flight engineer on a restored World War II Navy PBY, amphibious seaplane. The flight engineer seat is in the "conning" tower, which was the compartment between the fuselage and the wings. It is just big enough for one person and has two small windows on each side that are large enough to look out (maybe big enough to stick your head out). There is no window in the front, only instruments and controls.

We were on an early morning (7:30 A.M.) flight off the coast of Texas near Harlingen. We had ten people on board, of whom three were crew members. We had an AT-6 (old

[4]Graham, Billy, *Angels: God's Secret Agents* (Garden City, NY: Doubleday and Company, Inc., 1975), 164.

military trainer) escorting us and he was also doing some photographic work on our airplane.

We did a low pass over the water. Our pilot misjudged our distance over the water and hit the water in a nose down attitude. This caused the nose gear doors to rip open and act as a speed brake and catch water. The water caused the plane to explode; everything tried to stop at once.

The engines ripped off their mounts and continued to go forward. The propellers ripped off their mounts and continued to go forward. The cockpit completely separated from the rest of the plane and rolled under water. The tail section ripped off and rose into the air like a giant whale. This all happened in seconds.

I had no warning of this. No warning over the intercom. All I heard was a loud sound before I blacked out. I woke up in my compartment with only my head out of water, but water and fuel were pouring down on me and filling the compartment. Above this compartment was the wing and the fuel tanks, which contained more than three hundred gallons of gasoline.

It was dark and I couldn't see very much. All I could think of was that this was the end and I was going to die. I began thinking about my wife and daughters.

Then I noticed a bright glow to my left. The morning was overcast, no sun. There shouldn't

*be a light there, but I immediately turned to-
wards it. I don't remember anything after that.
I don't remember swimming underwater, which
was the only way to get out (I would assume).
The next thing I knew, I was sitting by myself
on top of the floating wing and above my compartment. There was not another person around;
there was not a sound to be heard.*

*After a few minutes another crew member,
the pilot, popped out of the water right in
front of me. I pulled him up on the wing with
me. His legs were broken in several places
and he had many other injuries as well. A few
minutes later, we heard someone else yelling
and saw one of our passengers back in the
tail section, which was floating about one
hundred yards behind us.*

*Only the three of us survived. We stayed
on the wreckage for about an hour and a half
before some fishermen took us to shore where
we could get to a hospital for treatment.*

*To this day, I feel in my heart that the
Lord wasn't ready for me to die and had other
plans for me. I believe that the light or glow
that I saw was a signal or a sign of passage
out of the wreckage. It must have been an
angel. If it had not been there, I would have
died. That was the turning point in my Christian work and activities. I will always do the
Lord's work and go and do whatever He com-
mands.*

Truth to Set You Free

How should we relate to angels? First of all, be careful never to become obsessed with angels. We must keep our focus on Jesus Christ, not His holy angels. But, perhaps you have been guilty of neglecting angels. Is it because of ignorance? Have you just been unaware of all that God's Word says about the ministry of God's mighty angels? If you have been ignorant, please repent of that ignorance. Put it behind you and accept the glorious truth of God's angels. The truth really will set you free.

Have you ever been guilty of expressing disbelief about angels? Do you still categorize angels with elves, fairies, and other mythical creatures? When you start talking about angels, many non-Christians will look at you as if you should be in a mental institution. We must remember that Jesus Christ Himself taught about and recognized the existence of angels. Jesus had personal encounters with angels Himself. To discount the reality of angels is to doubt the veracity of Jesus Christ.

The worst response to angels is not ignorance or disbelief; it is apathy. Could it be that while you believe in the reality of angels, you just really do not care? If that is your current attitude, you also should repent of that attitude and begin to thank God that He has provided these wonderful, ministering spirits to help us as believers. You should also ask God to open your mind and your heart to the presence and activity of angels around you.

Section V
The Message of Angels

Much of what people in America believe about angels is based on folklore and superstition, rather than on the Word of God. Many of the fantastic stories reflect beliefs in reincarnation or spiritualism. There will continue to be popular interest in angels and a profusion of books regarding them, but we must be careful to judge every account of angels in the light of God's Word.

We also know that angels have a wonderful ministry to us. Just as angels ministered with and to the Lord Jesus Christ, they also protect us and work with us. One of the main roles that angels play is that they deliver God's messages. The very word angel *(Greek* angelos*) means "messenger." Some time ago, I commanded my computer software program, "Quick Verse" to print out every verse in the Bible, Old and New Testaments, that had anything to say about angels—seraphim, cherubim, and spirits. I examined the resulting pages of Scripture and, with a highlighter pen, marked every instance in which an angel spoke. I discovered a pattern to the angelic messages that appear over and over in the Word of God. Following is a countdown of the top three most prevalent angel messages in the Word of God.*

Chapter 16

Afraid? Cheer Up!

The most common message that angels give us is, "Cheer Up." The way angels usually express this is, "Do not be afraid." Or, "Fear not." That's usually the first thing they say when they appear to people.

For example, when the angel appeared to Zechariah, he said, "Don't be afraid" (Luke 1:13). When the angel appeared to Mary twice, he said, "Do not fear" (Luke 1:30). When the angels appeared to the shepherds on that first Christmas morning, they said, "Fear not" (Luke 2:10).

When the angels appeared at the tomb of the Lord Jesus Christ and the women were shaking with fear, the angels told them, "Don't be alarmed" (Mark 16:6).

We see this message delivered in the Book of Acts. The last part of the book reads like an adventure novel as the Apostle Paul is on his way to Rome. There is a terrible shipwreck, but not a single life is lost. The reason is found in Acts 27:22. Paul was onboard as a prisoner.

Because the ship was in the middle of a

terrible storm, Paul spoke to all of the people onboard the ship, saying, "But now I urge you to keep up your courage, because not one of you will be lost; only the ship will be destroyed."

That verse certainly is of the good-news, bad-news variety. It is like the story of the couple who had a new car. The lady called her husband and said, "I've got good news and bad news. The good news is that the air bag works on our car."

Paul said that the good news was that no one was going to die, but the bad news was that the ship was going to wreck and be lost. How did he know this? "Last night an angel of the God whose I am and whom I serve stood beside me" (Acts 27:23).

When you belong to God and serve Him, God will be sending angels to speak to you. This is what the angel said, verse 24, "Do not be afraid, Paul. You must stand trial before Caesar; and God has graciously given you the lives of all who sail with you. So, keep up your courage, men, for I have faith in God that it will happen just as he told me. Nevertheless, we must run aground on some island." What are you currently afraid of? Are you afraid about what's happening in your family, in your marriage? Are you afraid of what is happening in the economy? If you will listen, I believe that God's message to you today could be, "Don't be afraid. Cheer up."

I have received a number of accounts in which people have had this positive message from an angel. I received a touching letter from a lady by the name of Pat Seale. She wrote about a time when she was a child. Because of a bone tumor in her leg she was scheduled to have her leg amputated. This is what she wrote to me in 1989 about this experience.

> My parents were consumed in their own problems. I know that they were torn up about me, but I still felt so alone. There was nowhere to turn, and I was only fourteen, so young and so scared. One night shortly before I went back to the hospital for the amputation of my leg, God did something very special for me.
>
> I had an experience so wonderful that it will live with me forever. I went to bed, but was awakened by something. I remember feeling so frightened. My room was cold and misty. At first I thought I must be dreaming, but I sat up and blinked my eyes again and again. I even pinched myself. I was very much awake. The mist soon took form at the end of my bed. It was a beautiful person dressed in all white. The fright I felt turned to complete calm. In fact, I have never felt that calm and peaceful since. He called my name and said to me, "Be not afraid. The Lord has sent me."
>
> Yes, I was to lose a leg, but I would not die. I was to trust God always and I would be all right. "He will take care of you."

He faded out of my room, and I was never afraid about losing my leg after that. I have done many things in my lifetime. I feel so privileged that God chose to comfort me at a time when no one else but him could. I still remember the experience as if it happened last night.

Another encounter by Velinda Ard follows.

Angel Encounter
by
Velinda Ard

After having an encounter with one of God's special agents, I know God sent this special spirit to minister to us.

On 21 January 1984, my son, Michael, was struck by a car on the feeder road of I-45 in Houston. He was thrown with great impact into the ditch next to the freeway.

A young boy his age (eleven) ran to my apartment and told me to come quickly because Michael was run over and dead. Fear struck me, for this was my baby. I was a single parent living in Houston, trying to make ends meet, and not in church.

On many occasions, my mother had told me to leave there and get in church with my boys and God would take care of us. Of course, I had ignored her warning and God's Holy Spirit that had spoken to me so many times.

But, this day I would have given my life to save my youngest son. I love him so much.

I ran to the scene and there he lay, helpless, as people watched and the paramedics worked with his young body. I begged God to please let him live and I would do whatever He wanted.

At that precise moment someone knelt beside me and in a soft voice said, "Are you the boy's mother?"

I said, "Yes."

He asked the boy's name then said, "Let's pray."

We, or rather, he did, and then he raised me up. I remember he took my hand. He was very tall with a shiny face like a bright light glowing and he had on a black jacket or suit.

After he prayed, he said, "Now, you go. Michael is going to be fine." As I turned to thank this man, he was gone as fast as he had appeared.

As we drove to St. Joseph's Hospital in Houston, I prayed to God to please save my son. We were told he was very bad and he would be lucky to survive. I called my mother once we arrived. She called the prayer chain of her church and they all prayed.

After spending the night in ICU, the doctors reported Michael was just fine and would be released in a couple of days.

Yes, I do believe in angels. There were those who could not understand it. My boys and I

*did leave Houston, accepted Christ, and be-
gan to attend church. God did supply all
our needs as He promised to do. I have told
Michael he is very special and I believe one
day God will use him in a great way to serve
Him, as he has such a beautiful testimony.*

*During those times when we are in the
storms of life, feeling discouraged, and de-
spondent, we should be still and listen. It
could be that we will hear the message of
encouragement. "Cheer up and don't be
afraid."*

Angel Encounter
by
Nattie Nicholson

*The day began on 6 August 1958, and we
were very excited over the impending birth of
our first and only child. After two hours of
waiting for the doctor to announce to me that
we had a healthy son, he called me into the
delivery room only to say that the baby was
not doing as well as expected. He indicated
that he had breathed one and a half hours
into the lungs of this child to keep him breathing.*

*I was told the next day (Thursday) that
the baby probably would not live. Then, on
Friday, I was told the same story. The baby
would not take nourishment and was failing
fast.*

I decided to make arrangements for burial. I went to the Memorial Gardens' office to purchase a lot, and as I walked down the street, I had this strange feeling, just as if someone were telling me to turn around. I did turn around and started back to my car, but turned again and started once again to the office. I felt as if I were pushing myself to go on.

To my amazement, when I reached the office of Memorial Gardens, the door was locked and not an employee was to be seen anywhere. I asked several people around and no one seemed to answer my questions as to why the office was locked.

Saturday came and I was told the child would not live through the night. Sunday came, and at 10:30 A.M. when I knew my worship service was about to begin, I entered my bedroom, closed the door, and talked to God, just the two of us. I heard this voice saying, "Cheer up, the baby will be fine."

In two hours, I had a request to call a certain doctor in Birmingham, whom I had never before seen. He came to the hospital and examined the baby for three hours on Sunday afternoon, 10 August 1958. I had the complete assurance before the doctor came that this child was going to live. God or this angel told me this. The doctor found nothing wrong.

That Sunday night, the child started tak-

ing nourishment, was completely well, and was never sick again during this time. Timothy is now thirty-one years old, has graduated from college, and is employed with one of the largest wholesale food distribution centers in the United States.

"Angels unaware"—I believe in them and I know one spoke to me.

Angel Encounter
by
Nancy Whittlock

God's angels are real. They are here to protect us, and really do; more times than most people ever realize.

My first known visit by what we believe to be an angel was when I was only seven years old. Being the tomboy I was, I had been swinging over a tree limb out over the sidewalk and back up onto the bank of the yard. I slipped and fell, sitting down very hard. I did not hit my head, just sat down hard.

In just a few hours, I became unconscious and was taken to the hospital. The doctors told my parents I would die, and for them to notify the family and friends that I would not make it much longer.

My mother wanted to be alone with me. While she was praying, a little black woman, whom mother assumed to be a housekeeper or maid, was there in my hospital room with her. She comforted my mother, prayed with her, and told her not to worry; the child would be better before morning. She left.

Just before daylight, I woke up, sat up in the bed, and talked. The doctors could hardly believe I lived because my spine had been bruised, which caused swelling of the brain.

My mother wanted to see the little housekeeper and thank her for her prayers and reassurance of my recovery. After being unable to find the woman, mother was told there had been no housekeeper or cleaning lady on the hospital floor at that time of night. Nobody else had seen the cleaning lady who had talked to mother and told her I would be better in the morning.

An angel had been sent by God to comfort my mother and let her know God was in control.

Angel Encounter
by
Rita Bryant

Early in 1945, my fourteen-year-old brother, John, suffered an attack of appendicitis. He was rushed from our home near Jefferson, Texas, to a hospital in Shreveport, Louisiana, fifty miles away. Surgery was performed. The appendix had burst, however, and infection had spread.

For days, John lay in a semi-private room

in critical condition. My mother sat next to
him in a straight chair. No one could per-
suade her to leave his side. She ate almost
nothing; she was utterly distraught and
spent her hours praying for his recovery.

Finally, when she was at the point of ex-
haustion, she gave in to my father's insistent
pleas that she go across the street to a little
hotel, if not to sleep, at least to lie down.

In the hotel room, she got on her knees
and continued beseeching God to spare John's
life. When she told of the experience, she always said, "It was as if a voice said, 'He will
get well, but it will take a long time.'" She
said that a strange feeling of complete relief
and calm came over her. She fell across the
bed and slept soundly the rest of the night.

Early the next morning when she returned
to John's room, my father greeted her with the
news that during the night there had been a
change in their son's condition, a "turn for
the better."

A number of problems and complications
caused John's recovery to be slow, but he did
live. Now, at sixty-two, he enjoys good health.
He and his wife walk six miles a day.

Mother lived almost a half century following her remarkable encounter. Sometimes,
when a person would wonder aloud whether
God hears and answers prayer, Mother would
say with a smile and great assurance, "Yes. I
know He does."

Chapter 17

Sleeping? Wake Up!

The second most common message that angels give in the Bible is "Wake up." Ladies, you are never more like an angel than when you punch your husband in the ribs during church and say, "Wake up!"

A good example of this "wake-up" message is found in Acts 12. In Acts 12:5–6, we read: "So Peter was kept in prison, but the church was earnestly praying to God for him." (Notice that there is a direct correlation between the activity of angels and the prayers of God's people.)

> The night before Herod was to bring him to trial, Peter was sleeping between two soldiers, bound with two chains, and sentries stood guard at the entrance. Suddenly an angel of the Lord appeared and a light shone in the cell. He struck Peter on the side and woke him up. "Quick, get up!" he said, and the chains fell off Peter's wrists.

The next few verses reveal that it is obvious that Peter must have been astonished by what was taking place. Because the angel had to tell him everything to do, he must have been speechless and wandering around in a daze.

We read in verses 8–10:

> Then the angel said to him, "Put on your clothes and sandals." And Peter did so. "Wrap your cloak around you and follow me," the angel told him. Peter followed him out of the prison, but he had no idea that what the angel was doing was really happening. He thought he was seeing a vision. They passed the first and second guards and came to the iron gate leading to the city. It opened for them by itself, and they went through it. When they had walked the length of one street, suddenly the angel left him.

As you read the Bible, you will be amazed at how many times an angel comes to wake somebody up. For instance, in the Old Testament, Lot and his family were asleep, and two angels who were visiting him woke them up in the middle of the night and said, "Hurry, get up and get dressed. You've got to leave here because God is about to pour out his judgment upon Sodom and Gomorrah" (Gen. 19:15).

Elijah was asleep when the angel came to him and said, "Wake up and eat." Zachariah saw an angel in a dream. Joseph, who was the stepfather of the Lord Jesus Christ, saw an angel in a dream. For some reason, angels frequently appear at night and sometimes in dreams. However, you should be very cautious about trying to find a message from God in every dream you have. Sometimes, weird dreams may be nothing more than the result of indigestion from eating cabbage and ice cream. Remember, however, that the Bible does say that sometimes people receive messages from angels in dreams.

I have received letters in which people have written about falling asleep while driving and narrowly escaping accidents. They recount that a voice suddenly woke them in time to avoid an accident. What is the lesson that we can learn from this?

Whenever you awake suddenly, pause for a moment and listen. I have no trouble going to sleep. I usually sleep soundly throughout the night, and wake up very refreshed. But, like most of you, there are times when I wake up suddenly in the middle of the night. For years, I didn't know what was going on.

Since I have done this study of angels, when I waken suddenly without apparent cause, I always listen. Almost every time, God lays someone on my heart that I should pray for. I listen and I respond, "I am awake now, God. Did you awaken me for some reason? Did you send an angel to wake me, to tell me to pray for somebody?" I start praying and sometimes I pray

for as long as an hour. I use that time when I
wake up in the middle of the night to listen to
God and to pray for somebody.

May I suggest to you who wake up suddenly
in the middle of the night, "Don't be scared.
Don't be worried." I challenge you to pray. It
is amazing how many times an angel will come
to us while we are asleep and say, "Wake up,
wake up."

Here are several modern examples of this
message.

Angel Encounter
by
Todd O'Neal

*I had an experience with an angel when I
was eleven years old. My family and I lived in
Tennessee. My grandparents lived about sixty
miles from us. One weekend, my grandmother
became very ill and we went to be with her.
After we had been there for about four days,
my father and I started home to get some
clothes and other things. It was late at night
and I fell asleep about ten miles into the trip.
My father was very tired from not getting
enough sleep and struggled to stay awake.
He fell asleep at the wheel as we were approaching home.*

*That night, I'm sure God spared my life as
well as my father's. I suddenly felt a hand
that shook me awake. When I opened my eyes,*

my father and I were going straight toward a telephone pole. My father was slumped over the steering wheel. I screamed and my father awoke and swerved the car directly onto the road.

I thank God for letting me wake up. I believe it was an angel protecting me.

Angel Encounter
by
Melanie Daily

I had an intense pain in the pit of my stomach. Mother drove me to the doctor and I was diagnosed as having severe gastroenteritis. The following day, Mother took me back to the doctor because the pain had not ceased and I could not stand up straight.

With a fever hovering around 103 degrees and a high white blood count, the doctor still insisted it was gastroenteritis, and prescribed a strong narcotic pain killer.

With the pain medicine and Mother's tender loving care, I began to feel better by Thursday afternoon. However, by midnight my temperature had topped 104 degrees and I was beginning to fade in and out.

Friday came and went as a blur. I can remember hearing Dad, on his knees, praying for God to deliver me, his twenty-one-year-old daughter. Friday night, no one slept, not even the dog. I had not been able to eat anything since Wednesday when the ordeal started, so I was weak and literally delirious. I was throwing up poisonous bile and would gag myself for muscular relief in my stomach.

Saturday around 6:00 A.M., I felt an overwhelming sense of calm come over me and my mind was made clear as a bell. I felt the presence of a spirit that spoke to me, explaining that I was dying and I needed medical attention immediately. Since Mom and Dad had been pleading with me for days to go to the hospital, they were very relieved to drive me. At the hospital, the doctors determined that I was in serious danger. They pumped my stomach and started an IV. Several X-rays and tests were run. The doctors came into my room for a conference with my parents. They had a brief prayer and rolled me into OR for exploratory surgery.

By now, they had no idea what exactly was wrong, only that I had so much bile and poison in my blood that I would die if they did not operate. An incision was made and every organ in my abdomen was carefully removed and cleaned. Gangrene had set in and a drain was inserted at my right side to keep further infection under control.

The doctors determined that my appendix had ruptured at least forty-eight hours prior to my arrival to the hospital. Another two hours, and I would have died.

Angel Encounter
by
Linda Robinson

In 1975, I was living in Utah, where I shared an apartment with a girl named Cindy. One night, I had gone to sleep early while my roommate was out. At around 2:00 A.M., I was roused out of a deep sleep by a male voice calling my first name. The voice repeated my name and said, "Get up and lock your door."

As soon as I was awake, the message was no longer audible, but the feeling was intense. I rationalized that Cindy would not leave the door unlocked. But, the message was very strong so I got up and checked the front door. It was locked. However, the prompting kept urging me to check the kitchen door that opened into an alley behind the apartment complex.

I froze with fear as I saw that the door which we rarely ever opened was, indeed, unlocked. So great was my sense of danger that I could not move. The internal voice almost shouted, "Now!"

I ran to the door, locked it, and chained it. Just as I did, I heard the sound of footsteps in the alley. Then someone tried to turn the doorknob. To this day, I believe an angel woke me, spoke to me, and then guided me to lock that door.

Chapter 18

Silent? Speak Up!

The third most common message that angels proclaim is "speak up." Luke recorded in Acts 5:17–20,

> Then the high priest and all his associates, who were members of the party of the Sadducees, were filled with jealousy. They arrested the apostles and put them in the public jail. But during the night an angel of the Lord opened the doors of the jail and brought them out. "Go, stand in the temple courts," he said, "and tell the people the full message of this new life."

Notice that the angel came during the night. This is when angels do much of their work. In the middle of the night an angel came, woke up the apostles, escorted them from prison, and delivered a message. He directed them to go, stand, and tell people what Jesus Christ has done.

As you study the Word of God, you will find that many times angels have told people to go and speak up for Christ. We learned earlier in this study that angels do not preach the gospel to lost people because angels do not understand the gospel. They have never been lost and thus never need to be saved.

It would be easier for us if God would just send evangelistic angels throughout the world to preach the gospel, but He doesn't do that. We are the ones to preach the gospel. Sometimes angels whisper in our spiritual ears: "Speak a word for the Lord Jesus Christ." That is what the angel told Peter, John, and the others.

Share Your Faith

We see this message proceeding in two different directions. First, a Christian may be directed to speak to a nonbeliever. In Acts we read that Philip, who was one of the seven deacons, was given a message by an angel.

> Now an angel of the Lord said to Philip, "Go south to the road—the desert road—that goes down from Jerusalem to Gaza."

> So he started out, and on his way he met an Ethiopian eunuch, an important official in charge of all the treasury of Candace, queen of the Ethiopians. This man had gone to Jerusalem to worship and on his way home was sitting in his chariot reading the book of Isaiah the

prophet. The Spirit told Philip, "Go to that chariot and stay near it."

Then Philip ran up to the chariot and heard the man reading Isaiah the prophet. "Do you understand what you are reading?" Philip asked.

"How can I," he said, "unless someone explains it to me?" So, he invited Philip to come up and sit with him.

The eunuch was reading this passage of Scripture: "He was led like a sheep to the slaughter, and as a lamb before the shearer is silent, so he did not open his mouth. In his humiliation he was deprived of justice. Who can speak of his descendants? For his life was taken from the earth."

The eunuch asked Philip, "Tell me, please, who is the prophet talking about, himself or someone else?" Then Philip began with that very passage of Scripture and told him the good news about Jesus. (Acts 8:26–35)

Have you ever looked at somebody and wondered if that person knows Jesus Christ? Did you hear a voice that seemed to say to you, "Why don't you speak to that person about Christ?" I have heard that voice many times. Whether it is the Holy Spirit or a ministering spirit, it does not matter. Many times God is trying to direct us to speak to people about Jesus Christ.

Look for a Christian

Likewise, sometimes a nonbeliever may be directed by an angel to seek a Christian. It is amazing to observe how God can orchestrate a rendezvous between two people.

Acts 10:1, states "At Caesarea there was a man named Cornelius, a centurion in what was known as the Italian Regiment. He and all his family were devout and God-fearing; he gave generously to those in need and prayed to God regularly." That is the description of a good man, but the Bible says specifically that this man was not a Christian. He wasn't saved yet.

Even today, some people think that surely they are Christians because they are devout, fear God, give money, and pray. You can do all of those things and still not be born again.

We read in verses 3–5:

> One day at about three in the afternoon he had a vision. He distinctly saw an angel of God, who came to him and said, "Cornelius!"

> Cornelius stared at him in fear, "What is it, Lord?" he asked.

> The angel answered, "Your prayers and gifts to the poor have come up as a memorial offering before God. Now send men to Joppa to bring back a man named Simon who is called Peter."

Do you understand what is happening? The angel directed Philip to go and speak to a non-believer. But, in this incident an angel directed a lost person, Cornelius, to go seek a Christian. He was directed to send for a Christian to come and share with him.

Why didn't that angel who appeared to Cornelius just say,

> Cornelius, all have sinned and come short of the glory of God? The wages of sin is death, but the gift of God is eternal life through Jesus Christ our Lord. And, Cornelius, as many who have received Him, to them He gave power to become the sons of God. Cornelius, if you will just repent of your sins, place your faith in Jesus Christ, and make Jesus your Lord, you, Cornelius, can be saved.

Why didn't the angel give that message? This is not the job of angels. One night, I was out visiting as a part of Continuing Witness Training. My partner and I went to a home and no one was there. As I was walking away from that home, I heard an audible voice as clearly as I have ever heard a voice. It said, "Go to the house next door." My partner didn't hear anything.

We already had a prospect card for the house where we had gone and found no one there. I don't often do this, but I went to the house next door, not knowing who lived there.

We knocked on the door and an elderly man came to the door. We told him we were visiting from the church and asked him if we could speak to him. He was very kind and invited us inside. We went inside and began to share the gospel with him.

The gospel presentation went so smoothly it was unbelievable. The man was hungry to receive Christ. We led him through the plan of salvation. He prayed and invited Jesus to come into his heart.

After we had finished and given him the tract, *Welcome to God's Family*, he said, "I want to tell you something."

His story was remarkable. He said,

> Last week I went to the doctor. The doctor examined me, X-rayed my chest, and told me that he found a spot on my lungs. I was so afraid. That night, I lay in bed and I looked at the ceiling and said, "God, I don't even know who you are or where you are, but I'm in trouble. Would you send somebody to tell me how I can get right?"

Isn't that amazing? We weren't even going to that house. We were leaving the house where no one was home, and it was as if God directed us to go to the man who had prayed that someone would come. Sometimes, God does that.

Harriet Renner's encounter is further illustration.

Angel Encounter
by
Harriet Renner

Several years ago, in the fall of 1983, my twins, Chad and Elizabeth, were four and attended morning preschool. Each day when they came home at noon, we had a ritual of deciding whether to eat lunch at home or eat at the park.

Many times we would choose to go to the park and we would usually invite some friend and his mother to join us. If the twins did not have a certain friend in mind, I would silently pray, "Lord, who would you want us to invite?" Sometimes a name would pop into my mind, I would suggest that friend, and the twins would usually agree that was just whom they wanted to invite.

On this one fall day, the above situation occurred, except for one main and thrilling difference. The twins were back in their room changing, so I was alone in the kitchen.

When I asked the Lord whom we should invite, a voice said aloud, "I want you to talk to who will be there."

I was very startled and turned around in the room to see who was in the room with me. No one was there, so I asked again, "Lord, who would you want us to invite to the park today?"

Again, the voice spoke out loud and said as if He were in the room with me, "I want you to talk to who will be there!"

Believe me, I was very startled and shaking and realized immediately that I had heard an angel's voice, or even the voice of the Lord. It was a man's voice, very strong and powerful, and I knew I should obey!

The twins arrived back in the kitchen all dressed for the park and asked which friend we were inviting. When I told them we were just going alone, they were content and ready to drive to the park.

Of course, I was very excited and nervous to learn who would be at the park, for I was sure someone who needed me would be there.

When we arrived at the park, the twins jumped from the car and rushed to the play equipment. I followed close behind them and was very astonished to find one of my very best friends, Sue Conner, sitting on a quilt, with her Bible in her hands. Her head was lowered, and she was crying and visibly shaken.

When I approached her, she looked up in amazement at me and said, "The Lord sent you! I prayed for him to send someone to me!"

She was going through some very tough times and needed advice, reassurance, and love. I could give her all of those, only be-

cause the angel sent me to her. I will never forget that day when the angel spoke to me.

*   *   *   *   *

We have had incidents in our lives for which we didn't know the causes. If we look back, we might realize that we had heard the voice of an angel. Another time in my life, it seemed as if an angel told me to speak to someone. I was a senior at Samford University in Birmingham, Alabama. My wife, Cindy, had already graduated from Auburn University and she was teaching school while I was finishing my last year of college. Each weekend we drove to Prattville, Alabama, where I was Minister of Youth at the First Baptist church.

One afternoon, we were driving down the main highway in front of the university and, as we were approaching a main intersection, we were stopped by backed-up traffic. About a quarter of a mile in the distance, we saw all kinds of emergency vehicles: fire trucks, ambulances, and police cars.

It is against my nature to stop and gawk at a wreck. I usually try to stay out of the way and let trained personnel care for the injured. I don't stop at the site of an accident unless I happen to be the first person there. However, as we stopped on that particular afternoon, a voice seemed to say to me, "Go up there. You are needed." I couldn't even see what was happening at the scene.

Let me pause here to give you a little background information. Cindy and I had hosted a weekly Bible study in our apartment. Some of the young people from our church who were students at Samford would come and bring their friends. One of the girls brought a freshman friend named Sandy. We became acquainted with her as she continued coming to Bible study.

After hearing the voice, I got out of my car and walked toward the accident. As I approached a bridge, I saw that a car had gone off the road, missed the bridge and landed in the water, upside down, with its wheels sticking up. Water was covering everything except the very bottom of the car and the wheels. I wondered how anybody could get out of that car alive.

I looked over at the fire truck and saw there, seated on the step, a weeping girl. She had a blanket wrapped around her, and she was talking with a fireman.

She and I looked at each other, and immediately I realized it was Sandy. The moment she saw me and recognized a friendly face, she jumped up and rushed over to me.

The fireman said, "Do you know her?"

I said, "Yes, sir. Is there anything I can do to help?"

The emergency medical technician had already checked Sandy and found nothing physically wrong.

She was immensely relieved that a friend was there to give her comfort and strength. I was needed. I had never heard that kind of voice before. It seemed as if God knew that I was there and that Sandy needed a friend.

That is really not the most amazing thing about that incident. Sandy said that when she missed the bridge and her car was falling into the water, she felt hands under her arms, pulling her out of the car.

The astounding thing was that neither her hair nor her clothes were wet. To this day she doesn't know how she got out of that submerged car, but she believes God miraculously delivered her.

You say, "Well, that is just coincidence, hysteria at a time of trauma." Sandy believes that God rescued her, and I believe that God gave me a message to go there and help her. Sometimes angels say, "Speak up." If you are listening, an angel may direct you to speak to someone.

Conclusion

Here are some practical lessons that we can learn from our study of angels.

One, be aware that angels are present. Hebrews 1:14 tells us that God has sent His ministering spirit to serve those who are heirs of salvation. Don't be paranoid, always looking around, but realize that angels are there. Chances are, an angel is watching over you at this moment.

Two, it is acceptable to pray for angelic protection. We do not pray to angels, but we do pray for God to dispatch angels to protect us, to protect our loved ones, and to deliver us. In the Book of Acts, believers were praying for Peter to be delivered, and the angels came in response to their prayers.

Read the tenth chapter of Daniel, and you will see an amazing truth about the relationship of prayer and angels. Daniel prayed and the devil fought and interfered with his prayer. God had to send an angel in order for Daniel's prayer to be delivered. It is an amazing account.

I pray for my daughters to be protected by angels when they are in school. Every time my family and I travel, I pray for God to send His angels to protect us. It is okay to pray for angelic protection.

Three, be kind to strangers. That is what Hebrews 13:2 says: "Be hospitable to strangers because some have entertained angels unaware." Sometimes you may have encountered angels and not even have known it.

Have you ever encountered an angel? Don't be too quick to say, "No." God may have sent a stranger to you and you simply didn't recognize him. Be thankful that God loves you and when you pray, "Heaven, help us," remember He may be dispatching His angels in answer to your prayer.

*We welcome comments from our readers. Feel free
to write to us at the following address:*

Editorial Department
Huntington House Publishers
P.O. Box 53788
Lafayette, LA 70505

═══════════

More Good Books from
Huntington House

New Gods for a New Age
by Richmond Odom

There is a new state religion in this country. The gods of this
new religion are Man, Animals, and Earth. Its roots are
deeply embedded in Hinduism and other Eastern religions.
The author of *New Gods for a New Age* contends that this new
religion has become entrenched in our public and political
institutions and is being aggressively imposed on all of us.
This humanistic-evolutionary world view has carried great
destruction in its path which can be seen in college class-
rooms where Christianity is belittled, in the courtroom
where good is called evil and evil is called good, and in
government where the self-interest of those who wield
political power is served as opposed to the common good.

ISBN 1-56384-062-6

How to Homeschool (Yes, You!)
by Julia Toto

Have you considered homeschooling for your children, but you just don't know where to begin? This book is the answer to your prayer. It will cover topics, such as; what's the best curriculum for your children; where to find the right books; if certified teachers teach better than stay-at-home moms; and what to tell your mother-in-law.

ISBN 1-56384-059-6

The Assault: Liberalism's Attack on Religion, Freedom, and Democracy
by Dale A. Berryhill

In *The Liberal Contradiction,* Berryhill showed just how ludicrous it is when civil rights advocates are racists and feminists are sexists. Now he turns to much more disturbing phenomena, revisiting such issues as censorship, civil rights, gay rights, and political correctness in education and offering commentary and punishment, civil liberties, multiculturalism, and religious freedom. Fortunately, the American people are catching on to the hypocrisy. Still, the culture war is far from over.

ISBN 1-56384-077-4

Can Families Survive in Pagan America?
by Samuel Dresner

Drug addiction, child abuse, divorce, and the welfare state have dealt terrible, pounding blows to the family structure. At the same time, robbery, homicide, and violent assaults have increased at terrifying rates. But, according to the author, we can restore order to our country and our lives. Using the tenets of Jewish family life and faith, Dr. Dresner calls on Americans from every religion and walk of life to band together and make strong, traditional families a personal and national priority again—before it's too late.

ISBN Trade Paper: 1-56384-080-4

Getting Out:
An Escape Manual for Abused Women
by Kathy L. Cawthon

Four million women are physically assaulted by their husbands, ex-husbands, and boyfriends each year. Of these millions of women, nearly 4,000 die. Kathy Cawthon, herself a former victim of abuse, uses her own experience and the expertise of law enforcement personnel to guide the reader through the process of escaping an abusive relationship. *Getting Out* also shows readers how they can become whole and healthy individuals instead of victims, giving them hope for a better life in the future.

ISBN 1-56384-093-6

A Jewish Conservative Looks at Pagan America
by Don Feder

With eloquence and insight that rival essayists of antiquity, Don Feder's pen finds his targets in the enemies of God, family, and American tradition and morality. Deftly . . . delightfully . . . the master allegorist and Titian with a typewriter brings clarity to the most complex sociological issues and invokes giggles and wry smiles from both followers and foes. Feder is Jewish to the core, and he finds in his Judaism no inconsistency with an American Judeo-Christian ethic. Questions of morality plague school administrators, district court judges, senators, congressmen, parents, and employers; they are wrestling for answers in a "changing world." Feder challenges this generation and directs inquirers to the original books of wisdom: the Torah and the Bible.

ISBN 1-56384-036-7 Trade Paper
ISBN 1-56384-037-5 Hardcover

Conquering the Culture
The Fight for Our Children's Souls
by David Paul Eich

Remember Uncle Screwtape? He was the charming C.S. Lewis character who tried to educate his nephew, Wormwood, on the art of destroying souls. Now, from a fictional town in Montana, comes a similar allegory. This compelling book is a valuable source of support for parents who need both answers and courage to raise moral children in an immoral world.

ISBN 1-56384-101-0

Global Bondage
The U.N. Plan to Rule the World
by Cliff Kincaid

The U.N. is now openly laying plans for a World Government—to go along with its already functioning World Army. These plans include global taxation and an International Criminal Court that could prosecute American citizens. In *Global Bondage*, journalist Cliff Kincaid blows the lid off the United Nations. He warns that the move toward global government is gaining ground and that it will succeed if steps are not taken to stop it.

ISBN 1-56384-103-7 Tradepaper
ISBN 1-56384-109-6 Hardcover

Anyone Can Homeschool
How to Find What Works for You
by Terry Dorian, Ph.D., and Zan Peters Tyler

Honest, practical, and inspirational, *Anyone Can Homeschool* assesses the latest in homeschool curricula and confirms there are social as well as academic advantages to home education. Both veteran and novice homeschoolers will gain insight and up-to-date information from this important new book.

ISBN 1-56384-095-2

Political Correctness:
The Cloning of the American Mind
by David Thibodaux, Ph.D.

The author, a professor of literature at the University of Southwestern Louisiana, confronts head on the movement that is now being called Political Correctness. Political correctness, says Thibodaux, "is an umbrella under which advocates of civil rights, gay and lesbian rights, feminism, and environmental causes have gathered." To incur the wrath of these groups, one only has to disagree with them on political, moral, or social issues. To express traditionally Western concepts in universities today can result in not only ostracism, but even suspension. (According to a recent "McNeil-Lehrer News Hour" report, one student was suspended for discussing the reality of the moral law with an avowed homosexual. He was reinstated only after he apologized.)

ISBN 1-56384-026-X

Beyond Political Correctness:
Are There Limits to This Lunacy?
by David Thibodaux

Author of the best-selling *Political Correctness: The Cloning of the American Mind,* Dr. David Thibodaux now presents his long awaited sequel—*Beyond Political Correctness: Are There Limits to This Lunacy?* The politically correct movement has now moved beyond college campuses. The movement has succeeded in turning the educational system of this country into a system of indoctrination. Its effect on education was predictable: steadily declining scores on every conceivable test which measures student performance; and, increasing numbers of college freshmen who know a great deal about condoms, homosexuality, and abortion, but whose basic skills in language, math, and science are alarmingly deficient.

ISBN 1-56384-066-9

One Man, One Woman, One Lifetime
An Argument for Moral Tradition
by Reuven Bulka

Lifestyles that have been recognized since antiquity as destructive and immoral are promoted today as acceptable choices. Rabbi Reuven Bulka challenges the notion that contemporary society has outgrown the need for moral guidelines. Using both scientific research and classical biblical precepts, he examines changing sexual mores and debunks the arguments offered by activists and the liberal media.

ISBN 1-56384-079-0

Hungry for God
Are the Poor Really Unspiritual?
by Larry E. Myers

Inspired by the conviction that the blood of Jesus is the great equalizer, Larry Myers set out to bring much-needed hope and relief to the desperately poor of Mexico. You will be deeply moved by these people, who have so little yet worship their Lord and Savior, even in the midst of their need. You will be inspired by Larry Myers's determination to bring not only medical supplies and food, but light and life to those hungry for God.

ISBN 1056384-075-8

The Extermination of Christianity-
A Tyranny of Consensus
by Paul Schenck with Robert L. Schenck

If you are a Christian, you might be shocked to discover that: Popular music, television, and motion pictures are consistently depicting you as a stooge, a hypocrite, a charlatan, a racist, an anti-Semite, or a con artist; you could be expelled from a public high school for giving Christian literature to a classmate; and you could be arrested and jailed for praying on school grounds. This book is a catalogue of anti-Christian propaganda—a record of persecution before it happens!

ISBN 1-56384-051-0

Handouts and Pickpockets:
Our Government Gone Berserk
by William P. Hoar

In his new book, William P. Hoar, a noted political analyst, echoes the sentiments of millions of Americans who are tired of being victimized by their own government. Hoar documents attacks on tradition in areas as diverse as the family and the military and exposes wasteful and oppressive tax programs. This chronicle of our government's pitiful decline into an overgrown Nanny State is shocking, but more shocking is Hoar's finding that this degeneration was no accident.

ISBN 1-56384-102-9

Gays & Guns
The Case against Homosexuals
in the Military
by John Eidsmoe

The homosexual revolution seeks to overthrow the Laws of Nature. A Lieutenant Colonel in the United States Air Force Reserve, Dr. John Eidsmoe eloquently contends that admitting gays into the military would weaken the combat effectiveness of our armed forces. This cataclysmic step would also legitimize homosexuality, a lifestyle that most Americans know is wrong. While echoing Cicero's assertion that "a sense of what is right is common to all mankind," Eidsmoe rationally defends his belief. There are laws that govern the universe, he reminds us. Laws that compel the earth to rotate on its axis, laws that govern the economy; and so there is also a moral law that governs man's nature. The violation of this moral law is physically, emotionally and spiritually destructive. It is destructive to both the individual and to the community of which he is a member.

ISBN Trade Paper 1-56384-043-X
ISBN Hardcover 1-56384-046-4